THE MAKING
OF STAR INDIA

ADVANCE PRAISE FOR THE BOOK

'Vanita Kohli-Khandekar is one of the finest writers on Indian media. This wonderful book is a result of deep research and is an important contribution to understanding the recent history of media in India'—Prannoy Roy, co-founder, NDTV

'Vanita Kohli-Khandekar is perhaps the most consummate ringside chronicler of the rise of India's broadcast television industry from the early 1990s. Since I too can claim to have played a small role in it, I have always read, with admiration and respect, her insightful journalism on India's electronic media. Nobody is better placed or more qualified to tell the fascinating tale of the rise of Rupert Murdoch's Star TV Network in India. Vanita knows the dramatis personae intimately—they surely must have trusted her with exclusive nuggets and anecdotes which are bound to make this book memorable. This one *has* to belong in any collector's library'—Raghav Bahl, founder, Quint, BloombergQuint, Network18

'Having been part of a show that turned around the fortunes of Star from a distant also-ran to the leader of the pack, my perspective of the broadcast behemoth remained sporadic and partial. This book fills out the big picture of Star as the dominant media player in India and tells the fascinating story of its successful growth in a racy, researched and readable way'—Siddhartha Basu, TV producer, *Kaun Banega Crorepati*

'This book is full of stories about the making of India's media industry from the lens of Star TV. There are plenty of tales that will make you curious, a lot of interesting Indian media and television history, and then there are those stories I'd label riveting. Vanita worked for many years with us in the media industry and remains a solid and trusted chronicler of the Indian media. And she's written four other books, with lots more stories. More than anything, I am very nostalgic about my fifteen years at Star TV, which built the foundation for what evolved into an adventurous and exciting media and technology career. *The Making of Star India* gives you a ringside view of how Rupert Murdoch's army of entrepreneurial Indians helped create this planet's hottest TV marketplace'—Ajay Vidyasagar, regional managing director, YouTube Asia Pacific/Google Inc, and a former employee of Star India, 1995–2009

THE AMAZING STORY OF
RUPERT MURDOCH'S INDIA ADVENTURE

THE

MAKING

of

ST★R

INDIA

VANITA
KOHLI-KHANDEKAR

PORTFOLIO
PENGUIN

An imprint of Penguin Random House

PORTFOLIO

USA | Canada | UK | Ireland | Australia
New Zealand | India | South Africa | China | Singapore

Portfolio is part of the Penguin Random House group of companies
whose addresses can be found at global.penguinrandomhouse.com

Published by Penguin Random House India Pvt. Ltd
4th Floor, Capital Tower 1, MG Road,
Gurugram 122 002, Haryana, India

First published in Portfolio by Penguin Random House India 2019

10 9 8 7 6 5 4 3 2

The views and opinions expressed in this book are the author's own and the
facts are as reported by her, which have been verified to the extent possible,
and the publishers are not in any way liable for the same.

ISBN 9780670090792

Typeset in Adobe Garamond Pro by Manipal Digital Systems, Manipal

Printed at Replika Press Pvt. Ltd, India

www.penguin.co.in

This is a legitimate digitally printed version of the book and therefore might not
have certain extra finishing on the cover.

To
Vijaya Khandekar and Suman Kohli,
the strongest women I know

Contents

With Special Thanks to . . .

My husband, Sreekant Khandekar, for holding fort while I travelled for research, for listening to my theories, and most of all for editing the first draft.

My son, Jai Khandekar, for putting up with long periods of neglect from Mummy.

Yash Khanna for always being there to answer any question I had.

Vivek Couto and Media Partners Asia for digging out and verifying any and every piece of data he and his team could.

Partho Dasgupta and the team at BARC India for their unstinting support of all my 'requests for data'.

Janine Stein of Content Asia for the hours of patience with digging out all the nineties' archives.

Sameer Nair for being the best fact and context check board I could ask for on Star's first ten to twelve years. And for sharing every phone number and name he could with me.

Shyamal Majumdar for allowing me to use the *Business Standard* archives freely.

Anurag Batra for allowing me to use the then *Businessworld* or now *BW: Businessworld* archives freely.

How to Read This Book

Many years ago, a senior manager in Hong Kong told me a delightful story about Rupert Murdoch getting excited over a cheap haircut in China. And about how the staff of the company stopped the enthusiastic executive chairman of News Corporation (now 21st Century Fox or 21CF) from going to a dodgy neighbourhood. Funnily enough, Murdoch is not a bargain hunter when it comes to business. He has no qualms about blowing up billions of dollars on his hunches and visions, much to the dismay of analysts and investors. In the 1980s, he bet on satellite television, and by 1991 he had almost lost News Corp to the debt that had piled up as a result. In the process, he created one of the world's largest pay TV brands, BSkyB.

Just when News Corp was crawling back towards profits, he went ahead and blew up more than $870 million on Star TV, the first and only pan-Asian broadcaster. When Murdoch bought Star TV from Richard Li in 1993, TV reached just about 200 million Indians. Now that figure is 836 million. More than twenty-five years later, with a top line of over $2 billion, Star India is one of India's three largest media firms with over sixty channels reaching more than 700 million people. In March 2018, it contributed close to 7 per cent to 21CF's $30.4 billion top line. 'It is one of our biggest growth drivers in the company,' said Joseph Nallen, senior executive vice president and chief financial officer, at a Deutsche Bank media and telecom conference in March 2017.

Murdoch didn't know all this would happen. What he saw and bet on was a large, educated, skilled population just freed from its economic shackles. He had just discovered Asia and knew that rising economies make for great media markets. Over the years, Murdoch probably learnt that they also need to be democracies—that is why in 2007 he finally gave up on China, a market he had long coveted. When India delivered on its promise, almost a decade after he had invested, News Corp became the cynosure of every media investor's eyes. This is the first reason I chose to write a book on Star.

News Corp was the first global firm to showcase the potential of the Indian media market to the world. Thanks to its play, New York–based analysts were closely tracking the Indian media market, catalysing several billion dollars' worth of investments. They still do. Go through dozens of transcripts of conferences and earning calls[1] between senior 21CF managers and analysts at Morgan Stanley, Goldman Sachs or other firms—India is always there. A hundred investor summits could not have done what one man's gut instinct did. 'Rupert [Murdoch] looks at business in such long cycles that people don't believe it. "Don't look at ten-year time frames, look at thirty-year time frames," he says. Because of this, his patience and appetite for investments are huge. We reinvest everything that we earn in India and that is why we have been able to build and grow our business so actively. No other Indian media company is in such

---

[1]   An earning call is a conference call between the management of a public limited company and investors, analysts and media persons to discuss its financial performance. It is usually held just after the results for a quarter or the year have been declared.

a continuous investment and growth mode,' says Uday Shankar, chairman, Star and Disney India, and president, APAC, direct-to-consumer and international, The Walt Disney Company.

Over the years, Star brought many things to India: Channel [V], India's first music channel, in 1994; Star News, its first news channel, in 1998; and Radio City, the first private radio station in India, in 2001. It also revived an ancient Indian game through the Pro Kabaddi League, and created one of the country's biggest video streaming apps with Hotstar. It resurrected Amitabh Bachchan's stardom thanks to *Kaun Banega Crorepati* in 2000 and changed the rules of television for good. It gave us Ekta Kapoor, and, along with Zee, kick-started the whole Oshiwara/Link Road–based Mumbai TV production industry.

The casual, confident, irreverent India on display on Channel [V] touched a chord. Star's first attempt at localization was a success. For a foreign company that was trying to find its footing in a nascent market, Channel [V] brought home critical lessons. Star learnt that the Indian market was about local content, local management and completely local thinking. It is a lesson Star has absorbed well from the start, which is why it is one of the most successful foreign firms in India. 'India is the only business in Asia where they are deeply embedded in the local content ecosystem and have a massive sports business. Other global-owned businesses in the region are selling Hollywood content through sales and marketing but don't have a large-scale local content business,' points out Vivek Couto, executive director of Singapore-based consulting firm Media Partners Asia. As Star's arch-rival and former partner, Subhash Chandra of Zee, puts it, 'They have done a good job not because of News Corp, that is the financial part, but because of our (Indian) people.'

That is the second reason this book interested me. Star has shaped the Indian media and entertainment ecosystem as much as it has been shaped by it. In 1992, India had an estimated Rs 1500 crore (just over $500 million) media and entertainment industry; today this figure is Rs 1,67,400 crore ($23.9 billion). If the story of India's media industry is told, Star would be one of the main protagonists. This book, then, tells one important part of that story.

There are, however, three things to keep in mind while reading it.

One, it was not commissioned by Fox or Star India. Nor was it suggested by or financed by Star. Except for legal head Deepak Jacob, the current lot of Star TV managers did not speak to me for this book despite repeated requests. However, the firm and its chairman, Uday Shankar, were aware that I was working on the book. Shankar even gave me one interview. I have been tracking the Indian media and entertainment industry, and consequently, Star, for over eighteen years now. I have been to their offices scores of times and interviewed or chatted with Shankar dozens of times. But for various reasons, possibly to do with the merger with Disney and the legal complications around it, Star chose not to talk to me for this book.

Two, it is not a comprehensive history of Star—that would require volumes. I have chosen episodes that define, illustrate and elucidate a point or a milestone—such as Channel [V]'s launch, which brought to the country its first local music channel, or *Kaun Banega Crorepati*, the show that changed the way we watched TV.

Three, everything that Star did or didn't do has to be viewed through the prism of the market, the societal background and the person running the business locally. The Fox structure is pretty federal; CEOs are generally free to do what they want. Each of the men who headed the India business have defined and shaped Star TV, as much as Zee has been shaped by its chairman, Chandra. Therefore, the book is broken up into sections based on the CEOs who ran the business over a period of time.

The question of what they achieved gets interesting reactions. While Star has been hugely successful in India, the value it built for investors is moot. 'If the definition of success is scale, market share and share of wallet, Star has done exceptionally. India will be the second-largest business that Disney will have after the US with the entire India business expected to generate a $2.5 billion top line in 2019. In terms of talent, they have a great team, led by Uday and Sanjay [Gupta, managing director] and various key people. Profitability has been a concern but what people forget is that Star has exceptional entertainment margins which it has ploughed back into sports. It has been a margin-depletive business but combined margins are running at 20 to 25 per cent. That is reasonable when you are competing with Amazon, Google and Facebook. Most people on the Street valued Star at $3 billion in 2006; by 2019, the valuation had reached $10–15 billion,' says Vivek Couto.

In 2018, a large chunk of 21CF was sold to the $60 billion The Walt Disney Company—this included Star India. By the time you read this book, Star would have become a Disney company legally and operationally. Disney paid $71.3 billion for Fox's assets. Of this, Star's value was estimated to be between $10 billion and $15 billion. 'Between 1992 and 2000, they blew up $2 billion on Star India. By 2017 this must be $7–8 billion. So a valuation of $13 billion is not great—that gives you an internal rate of return of 30 per cent. So the report on return on investment and return on capital employed is not great,' says one media baron.

Maybe, maybe not. But it's been one hell of a ride.

vanitakohli@hotmail.com
https://twitter.com/vanitakohlik
in.linkedin.com/pub/vanita-kohli-khandekar/8/99a/159/

Prologue

When: February–March 2000

Where: The office of News Television India (Star TV), Masterpiece Building, Andheri East, Mumbai

The Cast

From News Corporation (now 21st Century Fox)
Keith Rupert Murdoch, chairman and CEO
Chase Carey, co-CEO, News Corp
Bruce Churchill, deputy CEO, Star TV, Asia
Steve Askew, programming head, Star TV, Asia

From News Television India
Peter Mukerjea, CEO
Sameer Nair, executive vice president, programming

Raj Nayak, executive vice president, sales and marketing
Sumantra Dutta, senior executive vice president,
sales and marketing
Ajay Vidyasagar, vice president and general manager,
regional channels
Kaushal Dalal, executive vice president, business development
Arun Mohan, executive vice president, distribution
R.S. Narayan, chief financial officer
Jagdish Kumar
and others

The meeting was going badly.

Star TV's India office was presenting a review of its business to Rupert Murdoch, chairman of its parent firm, News Corporation. The first chart shown by newly appointed programming chief Sameer Nair had partner and rival Zee as the No. 1 channel with a 7 per cent audience share, followed by Columbia Tristar's Sony. Star Plus, News Corp's flagship channel in India, was a distant No. 3 with a minuscule 2 per cent viewership share going by TAM Media Research, the ratings body. Seven years after Murdoch had bought Star TV and poured over $1.5 billion into the promise of China and India, this was dismal stuff. Especially for an aggressive, ambitious media mogul running a $14 billion empire that owned some of the world's largest newspapers and TV stations. Murdoch hammered his hand on the table with, 'Oh my gawd! I never want to see this chart again.'

Nair moved quickly to the next point in the presentation. Star Plus was going to become an all-Hindi channel after the break-up of a joint venture with Zee that had restricted Star from doing Hindi programming. The big show that would lead this change was the Indian version of *Who Wants to Be a Millionaire*. Since Indians counted in lakhs and not millions, the show was to be called *Kaun Banega Lakhpati*. Nair was trying to get Amitabh Bachchan to host the show. The fifty-seven-year-old superstar was on the wane, his films bombing one after the other. Nevertheless, he was the biggest celebrity icon India had produced. Every Indian knew who he was.

'Are you doing the real thing or a rip-off?' asked Murdoch.

It was the licensed version of the hugely successful British show, said Steve Askew.

'How much are you giving [as prize money]?' asked Murdoch.

'One lakh rupees,' said someone.

'How much is that?'

'That is $2133,' came the answer.

'That is pathetic, it is nothing; what is the largest amount of money I can dream of winning?' he asked.

'A crore,' said Nair.

A crore or Rs 10 million is a huge amount of money for anybody in India, even today. Murdoch wanted to know how much that was.

'That is about $2,13,310,' said someone.

The bean counters in the room were beginning to fidget by now.

'Make it a crore then,' said Murdoch, picking up his jacket.

~

'That single decision is at the heart of where Star is today. It wouldn't have changed the industry the way it did if that hadn't happened. And Rupert doesn't get credit for that,' says Ajay Vidyasagar. 'Those few minutes is what made Star. Somebody had the guts and vision to ignore the prepared presentation,' agrees Kaushal Dalal.

Making *Kaun Banega Lakhpati* into *Kaun Banega Crorepati* (*KBC*) did not just treble the budget of the show, it changed the nature of the TV game in India. It meant announcing loudly, emphatically that Star was local, Hindi and very Indian. It meant using the Bachchan charisma to funnel audiences to *Kyunki Saas Bhi Kabhi Bahu Thi* and *Kahaani Ghar Ghar Kii*. It meant ruling the airwaves for six long years. And it meant that Star became one of the largest media companies in India—largely on the back of the headstart given by *KBC*. 'From a half-hour show to one hour, from a weekly to a daily and from a lakh to a crore in prize money, it was Rupert all the way,' remembers Sumantra Dutta.

Without Rupert, there would have been no *KBC*, and without *KBC*, Star India wouldn't have become one of India's largest media companies.

Part I

Richard Li (1991–93)

1

Once Upon a Time . . .

A young Chinese billionaire, a failed American satellite and a starved Asian market

Hong Kong, April 1992. Star TV was a fledgling outfit when the head of advertising sales, George Chan, called Richard Gocher, his vice president for international sales and marketing, and Gocher's junior Todd Miller into his office. Chan was puzzled. He had been told that Star TV had 'some viewers' in India. Miller recalls that Chan instructed them to 'go there and check it out'.

Chan's bewilderment at a viewer response from India was not surprising. To foreign eyes, the India of that time was closer to the 'area of darkness' described by V.S. Naipaul in his 1964 book of the same name than the major engine of economic growth it is now known to be. Indeed, just around then, it was nearly an economic basket case.

Just nine months earlier, in July 1991, India had nearly run out of foreign exchange. It didn't have the money to import even oil, prices of which had spiked because of the first Gulf War in which the US and its allies had attacked and destroyed Iraqi forces after they had occupied Kuwait. That month, the Reserve Bank of India (RBI) had to pledge 47 tonnes of gold with the Bank of England and the Bank of Japan to raise $400 million. India's nominal gross domestic product (GDP) in 1991was $275 billion—merely a tenth of the $2.6 trillion it is today. It was this near-catastrophe that compelled the traditionally closed, socialist Indian economy to begin opening up from 1991.

Two weeks after that directive from Chan, Miller and Gocher were in Bombay on a Monday morning (Bombay didn't become Mumbai until three years later, in 1995). They were meeting with about twenty executives from one of India's biggest advertising agencies, Lintas (now Lowe Lintas).

It turned out that the 'some viewers' Chan had heard of were actually several million. The folks from Lintas were happy to finally meet someone from the mysterious Star TV, but mildly miffed too. Their professional egos were hurt that Star had not found it worthwhile to even pitch to them for business until then, recalls Miller. This was the time when there was only one TV channel, Doordarshan or DD, a state monopoly. Airtime on DD was sold by individual programme producers. Star TV's channels were the first bunch of foreign channels that India had seen. After visits to Bombay and New Delhi, Miller and Gocher wondered if Star had hit a potential jackpot.

Though the Indian economy was closed, the advertising business was remarkably well organized and professional. That was because ad agencies such as JWT and Ogilvy had already been in India for several decades. Apart from the odd multinational marketer such as Hindustan Lever (now Hindustan Unilever), several domestic companies such as Godrej, Parle and Videocon were consumer-focused and made demanding advertisers.

On the media side, print, which dominated the business, was made up largely of regional publications; there were hardly any truly national titles. The English daily the *Times of India* was the leader in Bombay while the *Hindustan Times* was strong in Delhi. *Dainik Jagran*, a Hindi daily, was well-entrenched in the northern state of Uttar Pradesh, while *Dainik Bhaskar*, another Hindi daily, was powerful in central India. Feature film producers were many and prolific, and people thronged movie halls, even if the business made money only erratically. Electronic media was limited to the terrestrial, state-controlled Doordarshan and All India Radio (AIR). In a country with a population of over 846 million people, there were only 35 million TV homes, of which only 1.2 million had a cable connection. Till very recently, the reach for most media in India has been a multiple of five, the average family size. So 35 million TV homes meant that TV reached 175 million people, or roughly a fifth of the population then. And cable TV reached 6 million people; the exponential growth in cable households was still in the future.

Since the mid-1980s, operators had used cable to wire high-rise buildings, primarily in Bombay, playing pirated copies of Hindi films on video cassette recorders located in their control rooms. The Gulf War of early 1991 created huge excitement because it was the first war to be covered live using satellite technology. Indian five-star hotels bought dish antennae so that guests could watch the blood and gore comfortably from their rooms. Cable operators followed suit almost simultaneously. When Gocher and Miller came exploring, the Indian TV market size was Rs 496 crore ($192 million) in an economy that had just begun to open up. Of this, Rs 395 crore ($153 million) came from advertising and the rest from pay revenues or the monthly subscriptions we paid our cable operators.[1]

Soon, there would be millions of educated, middle-class Indians welcoming brands they had only heard about till then. There would also be entertainment of the kind a DD-fed populace could hardly imagine getting; that too as they sat in their own homes. Could Star

---

[1]   The dollar rate for the year being referred to has been used to convert the figures from Indian rupees throughout the book. In 1992, $1 = Rs 28.95.

capitalize on all this potential even if India was only an afterthought in its business plan?

A misfired satellite hits home

In the early 1980s, Hughes Space and Communications Group built three satellites for the Western Union Telegraph Company. One of the satellites, Westar 6, misfired after its launch in February 1984. It was stranded in low orbit until it was rescued by the National Aeronautics and Space Administration (NASA), refurbished and sold (by its insurers, Lloyds) to a bunch of Asian investors under the AsiaSat consortium for $120 million. In April 1990, AsiaSat1 was relaunched successfully from a Chinese rocket. One of the investors in the AsiaSat consortium was Hong Kong–based billionaire Li Ka Shing, who had interests in real estate, shipping and other industries. A satellite has several transponders which can be used to send and receive signals from space. While most of the transponders on AsiaSat1 were used for regional telecommunications, there were some left. What was the consortium to do with it?

Li Ka Shing's younger son, Richard Li Tzar-Kai, aged twenty-three, had just returned to Hong Kong from north America where he had studied at Menlo Park school, gone to Stanford (before dropping out) and worked for an investment bank in Toronto. He was now put in charge of the investment department at his father's company, Hutchison Whampoa. A decade in the US had exposed Li to loads of television. He knew that Asians had never seen the kind of entertainment that Americans watched as a matter of course. Most media markets in Asia were either closed or tightly controlled. And here was a satellite with an unbelievable footprint—it covered thirty-eight countries and about 2.7 billion people across China, India, Indonesia and Taiwan, among other places. It was safe to assume that there would be a demand for Western-style entertainment in these markets. Why not start a pan-Asian TV service, thought Li.

In the summer of 1991, young Li created Satellite Television Asian Region, or Star TV, under HutchVision, which was jointly owned by the Hutchison Whampoa Group and his own Genza Investments. This was, reportedly, Li's bid to make something outside of his father's rather long shadow.

It was a very different world in the early 1990s. Globalization was just an idea. Countries and markets could not easily connect with one another because there was no Internet or mobile phones. Even the World Trade Organization did not exist—it would be born on 1 January 1995.

So, exciting though it was to beam to a potentially massive market called Asia, the countries within it were hugely disparate. They each had different languages, different tastes and different regulations. The idea of cross-border TV was unfamiliar. Nobody knew which programming would work or what the potential was—in fact, nobody knew anything.

Li got to work, first hiring a team of advertising and media professionals from all over the region—largely expats from developed broadcasting markets such as Australia, New Zealand and the UK. Donald Atyeo was one of them. 'Neither Li Ka Shing nor Li had an idea of what exactly they were aiming at,' he remembers. By the end of August 1991, Star TV had started beaming five twenty-four-hour unencrypted and therefore free-to-air analogue channels—Star Plus (in English and Cantonese), Prime Sports, BBC News and MTV—across the countries that the satellite covered. About $120 million came in from advance advertising contracts and took care of some of the $300 million in set-up costs. Much of the programming was what the channels were airing in their home markets. This was done in lieu of a share of revenues or licence fees.

Richard Li's discovery of India

'When Star TV was created by Li [in 1991], the thesis was that they would aggregate the high-end consumers, the elite across the region,' explains Miller. To begin with, the focus was Taiwan because though it had a population of only about 20 million, it had the best penetration in the region with 5 million cable-networked homes. Besides, it was a rich market. 'India was not on our radar. We were pretty much told to "forget about India",' says Atyeo. John O'Loan, the man who set up Sky News, backs Atyeo up: 'Li had no idea what was happening in India. He was interested in China to the point that in a meeting he suggested too much time was being spent in India; China was the prize.' O'Loan was in Hong Kong to persuade Star to put Sky News on the platform, but BBC beat him to it. Sky News was launched in 1989 by the Rupert Murdoch–controlled News Corporation and was becoming a serious competitor to the BBC in the UK.

Then, two things happened at the same time.

One, Chan heard about the India numbers and sent Miller and Gocher there. As soon as Star TV made the first overture in 1992, the Indian advertiser embraced it. Godrej, British Airways, Amul Butter—Star TV kept piling up advertisers who were delighted to be talking to an audience other than Doordarshan's. Many came through that first visit of Miller and Gocher to agencies in Bombay and Delhi. Though Doordarshan did some great programming in those days, it was the only option. Advertisers enthusiastically started buying ads on MTV as well as on programmes such as *Santa Barbara* and *The Bold and the Beautiful*. These were B-grade American shows, but Indian viewers were mesmerized. The fact that English is an aspirational language in India helped them overlook the obvious blemishes in this programming. 'Star TV literally stumbled upon India. It was so focused on Taiwan that it had ignored this massive and diverse market. Then Sunita [Rajan] came on board and the team began to expand,' recounts Miller.

Sunita Rajan was a media representative for several Indian and international magazines such as *A&M* and *Fortune*. On a holiday to Hong Kong in late 1991, she visited Hutchison House at the suggestion of a friend in the ad agency business in that city. Star TV was building a global sales team under George Chan. In the course of interviewing her for the job of an ad sales executive, Gocher pointed out that she had no TV sales experience. 'Well, you won't find people with TV sales experience in India because there is only print and Doordarshan,' responded Rajan, who went on to become senior vice president, advertising sales, CNN International (Asia-Pacific). She joined Star TV in October 1992 and after a three-month trial moved to Hong Kong as part of the India-focused team. That is where she shared a desk with Miller. Both talk fondly of those days.

'We were selling an idea, writing the script as we went along. There was no satellite TV then. There were no metrics or empirical data. Who knew what was prime time, was it 8.00 p.m., 9.00 p.m.?' asks Rajan rhetorically, adding, 'Clients [advertisers] had no context of the environment beyond Doordarshan. We were not introducing them to TV but to options within it—international news, music, sports. Also, we were 24x7 and that was something the market still had to come to grips with.'

Not just satellite TV, but even the whole idea of sponsorship was foreign to the Indian market. Doordarshan worked—and still does—on a telecast fee model. In the early 1990s, a programme producer for, say, a series like *Circus* or *Dekh Bhai Dekh* paid it a minimum guarantee of anywhere from Rs 1,00,000 to Rs 5,00,000 ($3454 to $17,271) for a thirty- to sixty-minute slot. The programme producer then went on to sell the free commercial time that DD gave him on the show to recover his costs and make a little money. What Star TV brought was the idea of twenty-four-hour channels in different forms. For example, it bought rights to shows such as *Santa Barbara* and *Baywatch*, packaged them, put them on Star Plus and sold the airtime. On MTV, which was licensed from Viacom, it simply did the packaging and airtime sales.

Star TV was fuel for the cable fire that CNN had lit. 'The first target was affluent Westerners in Singapore, Taiwan, Hong Kong and the Far Eastern countries. That didn't pan out. But India worked because of enterprising cable operators who bought dishes and sold the signal,' says Atyeo. Every major business success is aided by at least a few happy accidents. But Star TV's fledgling success in a market 4400 kilometres away from the intended one—in India instead of Taiwan—surprised everyone. Within a year, Star was earning a few hundred thousand dollars in ad revenues out of India.

That trickle of money was the first thing that drew Li's attention towards India.

The second was a rice trader.

Richard Li comes to India

Subhash Chandra's journey from an eighteen-year-old who turned around the family business of processing foodgrain to the progenitor of an eclectic $4 billion empire is now part of corporate legend in India. He has guts, vision and a can-do spirit that is apparent even now at sixty-nine as he attempts to make a foray into politics. If he has an idea, he is willing to do anything, meet anyone to figure out what to do to implement it. And as luck would have it, he has had many ideas. He is a restless serial entrepreneur who had by the age of forty-one made a fortune exporting and processing foodgrain and set up one of the world's largest flexi-packaging firms (Essel Propack) as well as a huge leisure park (EsselWorld). That was when he, like many Indians, came upon CNN in 1991. He saw the potential for satellite TV in a media-starved market like India. He began a conversation with David Manion, president of Hutchison, which owned Star TV, to lease a transponder on AsiaSat1. On Manion's request, Chandra and his partner Ashok Kurien put together a show reel, which Manion liked. He suggested a joint venture.

Chandra and his team spent several months figuring out the legalities of using a foreign satellite to beam into India. Technically, it wasn't within the law because India's British-era regulation had not anticipated satellite technology. Chandra knew that sooner or later the government would have to open up the airwaves. The trickle of channels—CNN, Star Plus and others—would become a flood given how under-penetrated the Indian media market was. He wanted to get in before anybody else. Chandra and Kurien worked out a business plan for a 50:50 joint venture and assumed a transponder lease cost of $1.2 million per year (just over Rs 3 crore then), a figure Manion had quoted.

In December 1991, Chandra and Kurien flew to Hong Kong to meet Richard Li. The meeting proved to be a disaster. Li dismissed Chandra and said that there was no money to be made in India. Moreover, he wouldn't make the transponder available unless Chandra paid $5 million (almost Rs 13 crore) a year. Chandra was furious but gave in because he wanted the transponder. Li would still not sign the deal.[2]

The sequence of events after this is not entirely clear. According to Chandra, Li tried to hock the transponder to several media houses in India in May 1992. None of them—not the *Times of India*, not the *Hindustan Times*—were seduced by the enormous potential of satellite TV. Or maybe they were but they found the annual tab daunting because, at the time, media companies were quite small. For example, Bennett Coleman, owner of the *Times of India*, among many other media assets, today has a turnover of around Rs 10,000 crore (about $1.4 billion), but in 1990 it had a top line of merely Rs 120 crore or so ($66 million then). Another possibility is that at that stage, their existing business, print, was going to enter a phase of rapid expansion and they didn't want to take their eye off that particular ball.

While Li was still mulling over other partner options, Chandra took him around to show him what his Rs 1000 crore ($345.5 million) Essel Group was about. Essel Packaging, as it was called then, was one of the biggest flexi-packaging firms in the world. 'He [Richard Li] noted that we were supplying to Colgate, Unilever, P&G and many others. Richard knew these companies well; they were some of the biggest advertisers in Asia. The visit to the Essel Packaging plant clinched it,' says Chandra in his book. He signed a

---

[2] This is Subhash Chandra's version of this story, as told to this reporter in earlier interviews and also stated in his book, *The Z Factor: My Journey As the Wrong Man at the Right Time* (Noida: HarperCollins, 2016). Richard Li did not respond to my request for an interview.

letter of intent with Li in May 1992 and by October that year, Zee TV had been launched.

The Zee Group is now among India's top three media groups. 'Richard did not opt for the JV, but he kept an option to buy 25 per cent of the company [Zee]. This clause was only valid for one year from the date of signing and starting the channel,' says Chandra. Li did not exercise that option. The agreement had another clause: 'Throughout the term [of the lease agreement], HutchVision shall not launch, mount or programme any other channel which competes directly with the channel [Zee].' This meant that Zee would do Hindi programming while HutchVision would confine itself to English. This clause would haunt Star TV for many years.

The beginnings of Star TV India

The positive reports from his own team plus Chandra's obvious bullishness in spite of the lease cost of the transponder having been quadrupled probably convinced Li that there was more to India than he had given credit for. Soon, Siddhartha Ray, a tech-savvy executive who handled the media unit of the Dalmia Group, became the first employee of HutchVision India's liaison office in Delhi. He was hired as general manager, South Asia, in June 1992.

Ray urged two of his former colleagues from the Dalmia Group's (now defunct) print weekly *Sunday Mail* to visit Hong Kong since Star TV was looking for sales people. Jobs with foreign companies and trips to Hong Kong were rare in those days so both Raj Nayak (who later became CEO of Viacom18's general entertainment channel, Colors) and Yash Khanna went across. Khanna was hired and soon started the Mumbai office in the Diner's Business Centre. Though HutchVision was keen on Nayak, he was based in Bangalore (now Bengaluru) where it still wasn't ready to set up office. It was only about six months later when Nayak had shifted to Delhi for a new assignment that Star TV made him the offer once again. He joined the company in Delhi as areas sales manager for the north and east regions. Since he had worked in Bangalore, he was asked to service some key accounts from that region as well.

Ray's main job was being a distributor for Star TV. 'That was easy because cable penetration was increasing, there was unfulfilled demand,' says Ray. The big problem was advertising. 'Because of the Foreign Exchange Regulation Act [FERA], taking ads and billing was an issue,' says Ray. India was just emerging from a devastating foreign exchange crisis. It was paranoid about allowing companies—or anyone for that matter—to spend dollars unless it was absolutely essential. There were restrictions on the remittance of foreign exchange, which could only be routed via the central bank. Because HutchVision's was a liaison office, the company had to appoint a local agent to generate revenues. So, Mediascope, an ad concessionaire firm, did the billing for Indian clients and remitted the money after getting approval from the RBI, India's central bank. Multinational firms could book ads directly with Star TV in Hong Kong. Once the ad sales team with Sumantra Dutta, Khanna, Nayak and others was in place, Miller and Rajan stopped coming down from Hong Kong.

That this company would go on to become one of the country's largest media groups—by audience and revenue share—and remain there was far from evident. It was still the small liaison office of an English broadcaster which saw some potential in India. While there were several executives running the show in Hong Kong, 'Richard Li was very hands on,' remembers Rajan. In the first year, most employees remember Li as a benevolent owner who gave generous bonuses and rewarded performance. And the work was a breeze. 'It was an empty market so getting advertisers was not difficult,' says Khanna. He roped in MRF, United Breweries and dozens of other marketers who were willing to pay in dollars to have their brands appear on a 'premium' English channel.

The programming was largely reruns of American shows, music (on MTV) and whatever Prime Sports was running then. For many of us who grew up on Doordarshan's superbly thought through shows such as *Buniyaad*, British comedies (a staple on DD) and some outstanding European cinema, Star TV's offerings of *The Bold and The Beautiful* and *Santa Barbara* were somewhat cheesy. However, a large part of metro India, 'the English-speaking elite' as the ad sales team referred to them, took to it. And that worked very well for Star since advertisers wanted to reach this audience.

In March 1992, Raghav Bahl, a young entrepreneur who had set up Television 18, a production firm, managed to meet a BBC executive staying at the Taj Mansingh hotel in Delhi. He gave him the pilot of a business programme, the *Business India Show*. Around that time he also met Ray and gave him the pilot for a lifestyle magazine show. There was, however, no response from either until December. That was when Star TV and BBC commissioned their first local shows. Bahl's programmes, *The India Show* on Star Plus, and *India Business Report* on BBC, aired sometime in 1993. MTV too had one local show, *MTV Oye*, a Hindi song countdown much like *Chaayageet* on Doordarshan.

Meanwhile, China occupied Li full-time. The advertising account of Star TV was managed by the ad agency DDB Needham's Hong Kong office. Peter Mukerjea was handling the account. He worked closely with Li during those initial years. Li was finicky about the advertising going out on behalf of HutchVision, at times dictating the ads himself to the Chinese copywriters. People believed that the ads were directed at the Hong Kong government. Star TV could broadcast in Cantonese, which was spoken in Hong Kong and by a small proportion of people in mainland China. However, he wanted permission to broadcast in Mandarin, the language most widely spoken on the mainland, the market with a billion people. Till he was permitted Mandarin programming, Star TV could not hit the big numbers.

As a matter of policy, Star TV placed full-page and double-spread ads in international media publications such as *Time, Newsweek* and the *Far Eastern Economic Review*. The idea was to reach the international investor and advertiser community. In February 1993, Star TV reached 11.36 million households or about 45 million people in thirty-eight countries, about three times the number eight months earlier. The Hutchison Whampoa annual report was silent, however, on both revenues and profits. The business was eating up between $25 million to $80 million a year according to one estimate. To reach scale and profitability, Star TV needed a big infusion of money in both programming and distribution. News reports from that time suggest that investors in Hutchison Whampoa were getting impatient. This is what drove Li to look for an investor in Star TV.

Soon, Goldman Sachs was put on the job.

Part II

Rupert Murdoch (1993–96)

2

Rupert's Discovery of Asia

An Australian media mogul, a mad bet and an Indian marriage

On 27 July 1993, Peter Mukerjea returned his house keys to his landlord in Hong Kong. He was moving to Bombay that afternoon. Mukerjea had done three years as account director on the Star TV account at the advertising agency DDB Needham. He had just been appointed head of ad sales for Star TV's India business. Mukerjea had worked with Richard Li and his team; he knew the Hutchison system as well as Star TV. He was looking forward to his new role, especially the move to India.

It was a humid morning and he quickly got into a cab that would take him to Hutchison House. On the seat was a copy of the day's *South China Morning Post*, the leading Hong Kong daily. Somewhere in a page full of local news was a small item that turned his world upside down. 'News Corp Buys Star TV', read the headline. Mukerjea was stunned. Did he have a job? Should he move to Bombay? What would Rupert (Murdoch, the head of News Corp) do with Star TV?

That was the question everyone seemed to be asking.

The estimated \$11 billion[1] News Corp was (and is) one of the most aggressive media firms in the world. Murdoch, sixty-one then, had fought with governments, regulators and rivals to build an empire that had started with a single Australian newspaper and was now spread across the developed world. His firm owned the *Sun*, the *Times*, Fox TV and 20th Century Fox, among other assets. He was reviled by regulators and the media, revered by his managers and editors, and generally feared every time he entered a new country. He had upset the powerful trade unions in the British newspaper publishing industry when he switched from hot-metal, Linotype printing to computer-aided technology. This meant a lot of workers lost their jobs and the printing press for News International, his newspaper company, moved to Wapping, a part of London far from the then-publishing-hub, Fleet Street. The resulting fifty-four-week strike broke the back of the press unions. His newspapers sold millions of copies with their 'dumbed-down' or 'tabloid' headlines such as 'Britain's fattest woman ate a fridge and died' (the *Sun*) or 'Headless body in topless bar' (*New York Post*). Remember, in 1993, nobody outside of the US knew much about media barons such as Sumner Redstone of Viacom (which owned MTV) or Ted Turner of CNN. In fact, most media companies usually stayed within their markets. But governments were wary of Murdoch and the mayhem he could cause in a market in his quest for growth and profitability. He had done that in Australia, the UK and, later, the US.

And Murdoch was now on to satellite broadcasting. The first experiments with satellite TV had started in Europe and the US in the 1960s and by 1965 the first communication satellite was

---

[1]   Though News Corporation is a listed company, getting its revenue figures for the years prior to 2000 proved to be very difficult. This estimate for the 1992 revenues is from a thesis done by C.A. Mason and submitted in September 1992 to the Loughborough University Institutional Repository.

launched. Murdoch had kept tabs on all of them. Finally, in 1983, he bought Satellite Television, a one-year-old struggling pan-European broadcaster. It was renamed Sky Channel and launched in 1984 with a largely UK focus. Sky was broadcast over a C-band satellite. That meant cable operators needed large dishes, measuring two to three metres, to receive the signal and send it across to homes. However, the first experiments with Ku-band technology had already taken place in Europe. Unlike C-band, Ku-band is a more focused signal that can be sold directly to consumers, who can pick it up with dishes measuring less than a metre. Murdoch is widely quoted in the international press to have described cable and satellite television as being 'the most important single advance since Caxton invented the printing press'. In 1985, he renounced his Australian citizenship and became an American citizen in order to fulfil the basic condition for owning a television business in the US. He bought a clutch of TV stations, which became the nucleus for what is Fox Broadcasting today.

The very next year, he was blocked from bidding for a licence for direct satellite broadcast in the UK. It went instead to British Satellite Broadcasting or BSB. He then moved Sky to a Ku-band satellite, ostensibly to circumvent British broadcast laws. News Corp also expanded Sky's offering to four channels. The new Sky Broadcasting began airing in the UK in February 1989, before BSB, which launched in March 1990. By late 1990, Sky had 1.5 million subscribers and BSB had about 0.75 million. But it was clear that both competitors were struggling with debts and the rising costs of developing the market and selling a new technology that involved getting subscribers to pay 250 pounds for a dish and set-top box. That is when a 50:50 merger, BSkyB, was announced. It would market channels under the Sky name. Eventually, BSkyB became one of the largest pay-TV operators in the world with 23 million subscribers, 13.6 billion pounds in revenue and over 1.5 billion pounds in operating profits in the financial year ending June 2018.

That was much later. Before it started posting its first profits in 1992, BSkyB almost pushed News Corp over the edge. In the winter of 1990–91, News Corp was staring at bankruptcy. The company had a $2.3 billion debt that was due for repayment, and it needed about $600 million to simply get through the fiscal year. Murdoch had been trawling through the smaller cities of the US looking for investors and selling off a newspaper here and a printing press there to reduce debt.

That is why analysts were baffled with the purchase of Star TV. Why on earth was Murdoch paying $525 million—money he could ill afford—for a 63.6 per cent stake in HutchVision, a loss-making broadcaster that was neither fish nor fowl?

In February 1993, Star TV reached 11.36 million households or about 45 million people in thirty-eight countries. However, it didn't dominate any market and had had no success whatsoever in the largest one: China. In fact, it couldn't even broadcast in the language spoken there: Mandarin. For someone who had zealously guarded his family's control over News Corp's voting stock, Murdoch did give up a lot—half the deal was financed with convertible preference shares, which would eventually bring down the family holding in News Corp.

'The potential in Asia is enormous and it is obviously very exciting for News Corporation to be involved in Star Television. We will build a business out of Asia as big as two BSkyBs,' Murdoch was quoted as saying at the time of the deal.[2] This was Murdoch in his element—he'd seen something nobody else had, he was willing to take a punt on it, everything else be damned. That something was satellite television.

Rupert has a vision

Sometime in 1992, News Corp had a company off-site in Snowmass, Colorado. Many of the guest speakers that year focused on Asia. 'At that time, none of the senior people in News Corp knew a great deal about Asia, just stuff like population,' says Gary Davey, who

---

[2]   Luisa Tam, 'News Buys Star TV', *South China Morning Post*, 27 July 1993.

headed News Corp's first attempt at satellite pay television, BSkyB. The growth of the economy, Asia's commitment to education and technology, all of these were an eye-opener for the team. China, with over a billion people and a $445 billion economy,[3] was already attracting attention. The original Asian tigers—Hong Kong, Singapore, South Korea and Taiwan—had moved swiftly up the ladder and were being joined by a string of other countries in the region, led by Malaysia and Thailand. And there was India, with a huge population (846 million), an educated middle class and a closed economy that was just opening up. The promise of the continent was evident.

These were consumer markets that had begun moving up the income ladder; they were just discovering consumerism and wanting to spend. And a consumer market is full of possibilities for any media firm that earns money by aggregating audiences— either to offer to advertisers or to generate pay revenues. 'He was excited about entering Asia,' says Davey. News Corp was still largely dependent on newspapers though Murdoch had identified TV, films and entertainment as the next area of growth. 'In the early 1990s, it was all about satellite broadcasting. There were three or four companies and individuals who were very aggressive, but Rupert was the most ambitious and international in outlook relative to his peers. He was willing to bet and lose or bet and win. When he acquired Star TV from Richard Li in the early 1990s the two markets he cared about were China and India. He also tried to win in Japan but had to settle for far less in that market,' says Vivek Couto, executive director, Media Partners Asia, a Singapore-based consulting firm.

'After that off-site, Rupert was personally motivated about Asia. He discussed it several times. When the Star TV deal came up, we were at a point where we were determined to find the right opportunity in Asia,' says Davey, who was the first CEO of Star TV. He later became managing director, content, Sky.

---

[3] World Bank data.

However, one failed deal and another failed suitor would pass by before News Corp bought Star TV.

In the summer of 1993, just a month before the Star TV deal happened, News Corp was in talks to buy a 22 per cent stake in Television Broadcasts Limited or TVB, a local Hong Kong TV station and potential rival of Star TV. The sale was blocked by regulators because the rules restricted foreign ownership of a local TV broadcaster to 15 per cent. Then came the Star TV opportunity, which the UK-based Pearson (then publisher of *Financial Times*, among other things) was also chasing. Pearson had offered the Li family $625 million for a 70 per cent stake.

It was a tempting offer, but Pearson wanted a shareholder's agreement that bound the Li family in by making them retain a substantial shareholding till 1998. It saw Star TV as a risky investment for three reasons. One, a lot depended on the attitude of the Chinese government, which was also one of the investors in the consortium that owned AsiaSat1, the satellite Star TV was beamed from. Two, China was the single biggest market in opportunity terms. Three, China's size and the government's involvement with the satellite raised questions not just about China but also Hong Kong, which had been under British rule since 1841. This was due to end in 1997, when the United Kingdom would hand over control of the island to China following the end of a ninety-nine-year lease that had begun in 1898. Hong Kong was also where Star TV was based. The Pearson management probably felt that having the Li family in charge while the transition happened would be better.

Li, however, was not happy with the lock-in Pearson insisted on. He opted for the News Corp offer. The sale, for $525 million in cash and stock, was highly profitable for Hutchison and the Li family, who together had invested about $110 million in Star TV.

Murdoch was on holiday on his yacht, *The Morning Glory*, off the coast of Corsica, where Li met him and the deal was done. 'It was one quick decision. China had proven its might and India had just opened its economy. Li's Star TV was a modest operation which was still trying to work out a business model. We [News Corp] don't do much analysis-paralysis. We understand as much as we can about a market and then take a decision quickly,' says Davey.

In fact, News Corp had been quietly trying to understand India much before the deal with Li was signed.

Murdoch moves in

The doughty New Delhi–based Iqbal Malhotra has been a media consultant, market-entry specialist and producer of TV content for more than twenty-five years now. He was briefly associated with the setting up of one of the country's earliest satellite TV ventures by Ashok Advani, publisher of *Business India*, the leading business magazine of the 1980s and 1990s. Advani had tried to take his print success to the skies by launching a business news channel. A combination of over-ambition and poor choice of satellite led to a spectacular failure, bringing down even his print publishing business.

In March 1993, a relative in the legal department of Fox, Los Angeles, called Malhotra. 'They wanted some work done to understand how many TV and cable homes there were in India,' remembers Malhotra. As he got deeper into the assignment, he realized that negotiations were under way for the purchase of Star TV from Li. Malhotra had earlier looked into Star TV in Hong Kong and was convinced that satellite TV was the future. By the time the News Corp assignment came through, he knew the space. He became the India adviser for News Corp.

'I was giving Star inputs on India, its regions, languages and propensity to pay till July 1993,' says Malhotra. Once the first tranche of shares in HutchVision was bought, News Corp needed a strategy to deal with local content. While Zee was already on the same platform as Star TV, it checked out other firms too, according to Malhotra. Both Jain Studios and Siddhartha Srivastava's ATN did not work out. Jain Studios had started as a production facility for TV in 1991. It soon signed a joint venture agreement with a group of non-resident Indians and an American firm to launch satellite channels. It launched Jain TV, a channel focused on spirituality and teachings from different religions. By the mid-1990s, it had gone into other genres such as news, and in 1996 it listed on the Mumbai Stock Exchange. It remains a small player, with a revenue of Rs 3.17 crore ($0.5 million) in the financial year ending March 2018. ATN was among the earliest Indian satellite channels launched by Srivastava, who was then a cable operator. As far as I know the channel doesn't exist today.

Zee, the largest private broadcaster by then, used to uplink from the same satellite as Star TV. Its Hong Kong–based subsidiary, Asia Today Limited, did the uplink. That involves sending signals up to the satellite, which then bounces them back to earth for cable operators in different countries to pick up. The managers at Fox who Malhotra was reporting to were keen on investing in the uplink company. In their mind, Asia Today was the gateway, the company that finally beamed the signal into Indian homes. To Malhotra's mind, the real value lay in Zee Telefilms, the Indian entity that bought and broadcast the content, and he told News Corp as much. Asia Today was just an uplink arm.

'Nobody knew what kind of contracts Asia Today had with cable operators. It was a nascent market; nobody knew who controlled how much,' says Malhotra. India had 12 million cable homes by then and the market was growing thanks to cable operators, or 'cablewallahs' as they were called. Almost all of them were young men who had discovered a 'business' in flinging and fastening wires over treetops and buildings, installing a satellite dish and selling the signal it got. Zee TV, Star Plus and Prime Sports were all the fuel they needed. But these were small operators with a reach of anywhere between 500 and 1000 homes each. Their control over the last mile was tenuous. An unhappy subscriber could shift to another operator with just one phone call. There was no last-mile ownership, no regulation, and complete opacity about who controlled how many homes. And none of the money they collected went back to broadcasters. It was not a part of the business that News Corp could invest in with any degree of security.

Even while Zee and Asia Today were being considered as potential investees that could help News Corp understand and grow in India, the firm zeroed in on Ronnie Screwvala's UTV. It was one of the bigger programme suppliers to Zee. It was doing ad films, dubbing, making TV shows and doing post-production work. It had produced, rather successfully, India's first afternoon daily soap, *Shanti*, for DD. In February 1994, when Murdoch visited India, he hopped across to Screwvala's office at Shiv Sagar Estate in Worli and listened intently to a presentation on UTV. 'What they saw was a diversified media company that had execution and scale in TV,' says Screwvala.

A month later, Screwvala flew to London, met the Sky team, and soon News Corp bought 49 per cent in UTV for $4.5 million. By April 1994, Murdoch had also invested about $60 million for a 49.9 per cent stake in Asia Today, the uplink arm of Zee. And later, he bought a 49 per cent stake in Siticable, Zee's cable firm. The shareholders' agreement between News Corp and Asia Today stated that 'the joint venture would undertake programming in all Indian languages, while Star would remain only in English. This was to ensure that there was no competition between the partners,' said Chandra in his book.[4]

This is where the seeds of the conflict between Star and Zee were sown. News Corp was new to the market and Zee was new to the business. But even while it was doing a scan of the market, News Corp knew that going local was the only way to survive in India. 'Rupert understood that India has a literary tradition; that Western programming won't work. He knew that people have to be entertained in their own language,' says Malhotra. If that was the case, why did Murdoch concede the monopoly in Hindi programming to Zee? 'We knew original dramas was the way to go, but we needed to understand the market. We didn't have much of a management structure in India—putting that together took time,' explains Davey.

---

[4]   Subhash Chandra with Pranjal Sharma, *The Z Factor: My Journey As the Wrong Man at the Right Time* (Noida: HarperCollins, 2016).

When Murdoch bought Star he had a head start of at least a couple of years over any potential rival. But the 'no-Hindi' clause as it came to be known pushed it back by about eight years and eventually led to the divorce between Star and Zee in 1999.

Davey had already been appointed CEO of Star TV Asia in July 1993. Mukerjea had worked at terminating the relationship with Mediascope, Star's agents, so that Star could become a bona fide company in India rather than one with merely a liaison office. HutchVision was renamed News Television India Limited in April 1994. Rupert Murdoch was ready for business in India.

Going local

When Li sold HutchVision, every employee got a letter. 'It said that he had sold the firm and made money. And he wouldn't have been able to do this without the employees. To thank them he offered every employee of Star TV an option of five destinations: Bali, Koh Samui, Macau, Penang or Phuket. Every employee got a letter which they could take to the Amex office in their region, choose their destination and have an all-expense-paid five-star holiday for two people. It was my first foreign trip with my wife,' remembers Raj Nayak, then regional head of ad sales for Star TV for the north and east based out of Delhi. Nayak was the star salesman and would later become one of India's most high-profile media executives. The gentle days of being a liaison office, however, were coming to an end.

'Once Rupert bought the business, it changed, became more aggressive,' says Megha Tata, then ad sales coordinator in Bombay, who went on to become the managing director, South Asia, for HBO and more recently Discovery Communications. 'They understood the business, brought in people with TV experience from international markets to share best practices,' says Nayak. And most importantly, Star, unlike any other foreign broadcaster then, actively sought and hired local management. It is a tradition that stood it in good stead over the next two decades.

Its first test came when MTV walked out of the Star bouquet.

3

Murugun Shoots for Murdoch

Music, Hinglish, Ruby Bhatia, Lucky Ali and the making of a subculture

Have you ever wondered why Indian films have so many songs and dances?

Our storytelling tradition across generations has been 'musical'—a combination of the spoken word, song and dance. This carried forth into popular cinema and, later, television. Back in 1913, most Indians did not see the point of the on-screen explanatory texts in India's first film, *Raja Harishchandra*. They knew the verses and could sing along. I am part of the generation that waited for *Chaayageet*, a countdown of songs on DD that was the weekly highlight of our humdrum middle-class lives. Most of us grew up playing *antakshari*.[1]

---

[1] Antakshari is a game that almost everybody in India plays at some point or the other. There are usually two teams. Each has to sing a song starting with the last syllable of the song sung by the opposing team.

When Viacom's MTV came to India along with Star TV in 1991, its competition was *Chaayageet* on DD, the odd cable channel playing film songs, music on the state-controlled AIR and of course the music sold on cassettes. MTV didn't realize it, but it was talking to an audience that loved its music, understood it and had strong views on it. Its American music found favour in urban India, the first bastion of cable growth. However, the big market for music was (and is) in Hindi, Tamil, Telugu, Malayalam and all the Indian languages that truly satisfy our need for entertainment. More than 90 per cent of all music heard, sold and enjoyed then was film music.[2]

Donald Atyeo, who was part of the original Star TV team and moved to News Corp when it bought Star TV, says, 'We kept pressuring MTV to localize more. Their only interest was in recycling the material they already had. They didn't want to localize because they would have had to invest. We broke the rules by doing *MTV Oye* [with Anu Agarwal]. We realized that in China, Taiwan and India, Western music was very small.' *MTV Oye,* which came around the beginning of 1994, gave Indians a taste of a snappily put together music countdown with video jockeys (VJs), the works. By April 1994 the friction between Star TV and MTV, owned by firms that were bitter rivals in their home market in the US, had become severe. MTV was part of the Star TV bouquet in Asia under a franchisee arrangement. 'The contract said if ownership [of HutchVision] changed, MTV could renegotiate the contract,' says Atyeo. When News Corp bought the firm in July 1993, ownership changed. That, it seems, is what MTV used to get out of the arrangement.

Another technological development at around the same time had a bearing on the course that Star took—the satellite beam for Star was split into two: a northern one targeting China and a southern one focused on India. It was simply chance that this happened

---

[2]   The proportion is close to 70 per cent now, but film music continues to dominate the Indian music market.

around the time MTV decided to leave. But it meant that Star could do a more focused, India-specific music channel instead of the pan-Asian fare that MTV offered. With MTV due to leave the fold in six weeks, Atyeo put together a team to launch a music channel that he thought would work in this market. And that's how India's first music channel—Channel [V]—was born. It began as a 50:50 joint venture between News Corp and four music companies—Sony Pictures Entertainment, Warner Music Group, EMI Music and BMG Ariola Musik, a unit of Bertelsmann AG. Together, these four firms invested about $50 million in the joint venture.

We are like this only

Shashanka Ghosh is a creative guy in the old mould, the kind you read about in advertising bestsellers. He is wacky, brilliant, impossible to pin down and someone who dances to his own tune. At some point in 1993, as an adman with JWT, Hong Kong, Ghosh together with (now investor) Mahesh Murthy and (now film-maker) Rakesh Mehra sent some promo shorts to MTV for a lark. They loved them and he was hired for MTV Bombay. Ghosh's shorts stood out for their ability to bring out uniquely Indian aspects of life that helped promote this all-American brand—MTV. So whether it was a dosa being tossed in the air or an ear cleaner doing his thing, his promos invariably made viewers laugh. He also started designing shows for MTV including its first local show, *MTV Oye*, a 'huge success', says Ghosh, now among India's top film-makers.

At some point in 1994 his boss Steve Grieder, creative director at MTV Asia, called to say that MTV and Star were splitting up. Ghosh and Grieder landed up on the Star side along with another MTV man, Ed Sharples. In the summer of 1994, when the break-up happened, Atyeo hired Sharples as general manager, packed him off to India and asked him to launch a music channel with a sharp deadline: four weeks. At midnight on 23 May 1994, the proposed Channel X would replace MTV. That, incidentally, was the music channel's name for the first three weeks in the making.

The story goes that Murdoch was against that title because his first failure was a Channel X.[3] So it became Channel [V]. 'Steve's contribution was the brackets,' guffaws Ghosh. Channel [V] was India's first home-grown, feet-on-the ground, head-all-over-the-world music channel.

Sharples, Ghosh and the rest of the team worked out of the residential floors in Shelley's Hotel in Colaba, Bombay. They found interesting VJs in Ms India–Canada Ruby Bhatia, model Sophia Haque and actor Javed Jaffrey, among many others. This was a young, fresh and 'with-it' breed of Indians who spoke the language that we, who were just beginning our working lives or teenage years, spoke in the 1990s. 'We wanted to play Hindi music and put it in an environment where it was cool to sing Hindi songs,' explains Sharples. He would go out with Bhatia or one of the VJs, shoot links and 'then go around to music companies and look for stuff from their libraries. We wanted more local music, songs from movies or clips that viewers wanted,' says Sharples. Only about a fifth of Channel [V]'s programming was Western music, most of it was local and about half of that was film music.

This, says Mandar Thakur, who joined as music and artiste relations manager in 1995, was the first of the three pivots that Channel [V]'s success rested on—the localization of the programming and its look and feel, the push for Hindi pop and combining its on- and off-air approach.

Take the first. The vibe of the channel was fresh and eclectic. It was a blend of India and the West, a look at how the country saw itself and the rest of the world. Ghosh's promos spoke a new language of Indian imagery, irreverence and fun, creating their own subculture. 'The brief was to do promos that demonstrated Channel [V] was clearly Indian,' says Ghosh, who is known to this day for his work on Channel [V] and for the tagline, 'We are like this only.'

---

[3]   There is no way of verifying this story since Rupert Murdoch did not respond to my request for an interview for this book.

A few months after the launch when Rajesh Devraj, a writer and a friend, showed Ghosh some sketches of Quick Gun Murugan, the ultimate Curry Western character was born.[4] 'What Channel [V] did is say that it is cool to be a Hindi-speaking teenager. Our VJs spoke a mixture of Hindi and English [called Hinglish],' says Sharples. 'We were getting India into Indian TV,' adds Ghosh. For instance, Indian videos were treated on par with foreign ones. So, right after a Madonna song, a VJ might say, 'And now here is the hit single from the Madonna of India, Alisha Chinai.' Her single 'Made in India' was a rage at that time.

That brings us to the second pivot Thakur highlights—the push for Hindi pop, a moribund genre that had found no platform until then. Channel [V] breathed life into this genre. Some of the newer music companies then such as Magnasound and Crescendo 'were spewing out artistes like crazy because Channel [V] was here. We were being bombarded with music videos,' says Thakur. In those days, without data analytics or a strong feedback loop, choosing the video was simple. 'If all of us liked it, we promoted it. Today's culture is more about discovery and recommendation,' reckons Thakur, who is now chief operating officer (COO) at Times Music.

There were no other music channels, no private or FM radio and certainly no Internet. Among the non-film singers Channel [V] brought in were many British-Asians—Bally Sagoo, Apache Indian. They, along with Chinai, Lucky Ali and Daler Mehndi, brought new sounds to India and soon many of them became very successful in mainstream film music too.

The third pivot, says Thakur, was unifying what Channel [V] did on the ground with events and shows and what it did on-air. For example, the *Bacardi Blast* show became a tour that was replicated in twenty cities across the country. There was the Channel [V] Diva Awards with the Indian Music Industry's association. 'Every big star has played there, Spice Girls, Bon Jovi. Remember, this

---

[4] Quick Gun Murugan's immense popularity spawned a film by the same name that Shashanka Ghosh directed. It was released in 2009.

was a time when, except for the Filmfare awards, there were no major entertainment-oriented awards in India. The Channel [V] roadshows generated both programming and huge amounts of buzz,' says Thakur. Most media companies did not do this. Many would have an event that would find a mention somewhere. But combining it all in one 360-degree swathe where the content and its coverage was across media meant advertisers got better value for money.

In the media-barren landscape of 1994, Channel [V] was a spectacular overnight success—something Star had not experienced anywhere else in Asia. Atyeo savours the moment: 'It was extraordinary; I can't believe how quickly we became popular. We were just there at the right time. When we started *BPL Oye* we were the No. 1 channel other than DD. It was gratifying. We were also told that we were a corrupting influence. We got a lot of letters from parents nervous about the channel's effect on kids.'

Adds Sharples, 'We realized we were on to something because of the feedback. This was before mobile phones and SMS—so this was from the letters we received, from people we met, from advertisers.' One of those letters was from a tailor in Delhi. His business was booming because people wanted copies of the outfits VJs such as Bhatia were wearing. But he had a request: could Channel [V] get them to spin around so that he could copy the back of the outfit properly?

In September 1994, Atyeo asked Sunita Rajan to come to Bombay as the regional sales manager and monetize the channel. This was the time when brands such as Coca-Cola and Kellogg's were entering India and domestic names such as BPL and Videocon were seeking to expand sales dramatically in an economy that was opening up. Channel [V] matched the mood of a young nation looking towards the world. 'It was magical,' says Rajan. Every show they launched found an instant sponsor. The first big one was consumer electronics brand BPL. 'They paid us more than $1 million for one year for a weekly Monday night show, a mix of Hindi and pop, archival and current,' says Rajan. Thus came about *BPL Oye,* followed by *Timex Timepass* and *Videocon Mangta Hai,* among many others. 'It was the branded content of those days,' explains Rajan.

'Mandar [Thakur] and [Luke] Kenny[5] were able to feel the pulse. If the head of a business we were pitching to had a sense for music, they bought into it. The Dhoots [who own Videocon] loved music, especially old music, and they loved Javed Jaffrey. So we took him along to the meeting,' remembers Rajan. And that was how *Videocon Flashback* came into existence.

Jules Fuller, till late 2018 the head of special projects at Endemol UK, joined Channel [V] in November 1994, six months after its launch. 'There was an incredible amount of energy and creative talent. Shashanka, Shamin Desai, Rajesh Devraj, it was a hotbed of talent,' he says. Ghosh, Sharples, Rajan, Thakur, Desai,[6] each of the people credited with building Channel [V], went on to bigger things and greater success.

The creative and commercial chops that the team displayed caused some heartburn. 'We were the envy of the Star TV team because we used to get a lot of press. We would deliberately make a lot of noise and ensure that our VJs' and channel's name was in the papers,' laughs Rajan. 'We made money within the first two years,' adds Fuller. Not a lot though, since music is not a very big or lucrative genre in India. According to one estimate, Channel [V] did about Rs 50 crore (about $12–13 million) in revenue at its peak.

New York takes note

The buzz hit Hong Kong and then New York when Asian and Western newspapers and magazines started looking at what made Channel [V] tick. It made the top brass at the News Corp headquarters in New York sit up and take notice.

Star's first big success in India was notable for three reasons.

---

[5] Mandar Thakur and Luke Kenny were part of the Channel [V] team then. Luke Kenny was a VJ and has acted in several films.

[6] Shamin Desai died in 2011.

One, it clearly showed that local was the way to go. It gave Star the direction that most foreign companies trying to find their feet in a nascent market seek. This was especially valuable in the pre-Internet and telecom days when information took time to travel. 'Rupert came over often but he was more interested in China—China was the bigger deal. But India was starting to boom, too,' remembers Atyeo. It was late in 1995, soon after Channel [V]'s success, that the point hit home. This was in a meeting set up by Gary Davey, Star TV's CEO then. 'India was fast becoming Star's main market and the meeting was designed to "educate" the Murdochs and a bunch of News Corp bean counters from New York about the opportunities there and to devise a strategy to fulfil them. It was held in Hong Kong, so a number of Star employees from India were flown in,' says Atyeo. The story of this meeting is worth knowing to gain an insight into Murdoch's mind.

Rakesh Sharma had joined Channel [V] in 1994 and then moved on to become head of Star Plus. He is one of India's best documentary film-makers. By then he had done documentaries and assisted on the iconic fifty-three-episode *The Discovery of India*, a TV show based on a book by India's first prime minister, Jawaharlal Nehru. Sharma is a contrarian, has always been. So when he was asked to wear formals for the Hong Kong meeting, he wore a brick-red Fabindia kurta pyjama, which passes for Indian formals. Sharma, who remembers the meeting, laughs while describing it. 'There were about ten people. Murdoch was right across from me at this rectangular table. In a sea of suits was this blood-red kurta, and he was fixated on me. He asked me what I do. I told him I was tasked with the Indianization of Star.' After that the entire meeting went out of the window.

'Within the first minute he started asking me about other things. We talked of politics, government, consumer banks, agrarian banks,' says Sharma, who had travelled a fair bit in Punjab, Uttar Pradesh, Rajasthan and Bihar, among other parts of the country. His perspective was totally different from that of teams that had known only Delhi, Mumbai or Hong Kong. The first satellite television experiments were undertaken by DD as early as 1975–76. It was under the Satellite Instructional Television Experiment (SITE) that the Indian government used NASA's Satellite ATS-6 for educational programme broadcasts in Indian villages. Sharma talked about that, about community TV and how it worked. The discussion turned to whether Star could be installing community TVs in B- and C-class towns with one-lakh-plus populations. 'We were tossing ideas on distribution. He was interested in knowing things that could help him expand and get in before competition did,' says Sharma. The chat lasted for two hours, says Atyeo. 'Rakesh pretty much stole the show. Us Europeans didn't get a look in, no matter how much time we'd spent in India. At one point Rupert turned a baleful eye on me and said, "With all due respect, Mr Atyeo, what do you know about India?" Fortunately, Andrew Carnegie [general manager for India] came to my rescue and told him that it was the music channel which had pioneered local Indian content for Star, so I kept my job. Anyway, after that meeting India became the major focus for Star. All down to Rakesh looking like an ad for Fabindia!' laughs Atyeo.

One of the big things that sank into the minds of the top brass then was that India had a robust content ecosystem thanks to its film industry, and the fact that it was a democracy. The absence of these two factors was among the main reasons why Star eventually gave up on China.

That brings us to the second reason the Channel [V] story is significant. Not just the content ecosystem, Channel [V]'s success also brought to News Corp's attention the strength of local management. People like Rajan and Ghosh were native Indians who were working abroad because there weren't enough opportunities at home. But given the chance in their home markets they did wonders with Channel [V]. It pushed Star to do the one thing that made it more successful than any of its American contemporaries— hire strong local managers and give them freedom right from the outset. This created its own problems, say several of the Indian managers—such as Sharma—from the early 1990s. Many of the English and Australian middle managers didn't think the 'natives' could run things. Also, there were many who were openly racist and patronizing and assumed that Indians didn't know anything about, say, Arnold Schwarzenegger or a Hollywood film, and it was Star's job was to offer that.

Three, Channel [V] showed a young, casual, irreverent India that was confident and could laugh at itself, a quality that was missing in most mass media entertainment. There were films that reflected our times. But most of the music on TV was a linear listing kind of play. There was no context, no rationale, because that was the nature of the market. We didn't expect any better, we hadn't seen any better. Channel [V][7] brought a bhelpuri of pop culture, Indian music, Western sensibilities, Hinglish and global characters as VJs. In the process it created a subculture that endured and defined what MTV and dozens of other channels did later.

'Channel [V]'s wild success emboldened us,' sums up Sumantra Dutta, then part of the Star TV ad sales team. John O'Loan, (then) executive vice president, Star TV, says, 'It was a turning point.'

And one that led to a very bumpy road.

---

[7] After various failed permutations and combinations, Channel [V] was shut down in November 2017.

Part III

Rathikant Basu (1996–99)

4

The First CEO

A bureaucrat, a state-owned broadcaster, satellites in the sky and Prannoy Roy

In May 1993, just a couple of months before Rupert Murdoch bought a majority stake in Star TV, Rathikant Basu, a fifty-something Indian Administrative Service (IAS) officer, took over as director general of a floundering DD. Neither knew the other, but their paths would cross soon. So would those of the Indian government and Murdoch.

For too long, the government had ruled the Indian airwaves with DD and AIR. The rise of private broadcasting had made officialdom distinctly uncomfortable, and the government spent much of the 1990s trying to stifle it rather than facilitate it and treat it as a generator of jobs, income and taxes. As long as Richard Li, the son of a Chinese billionaire, owned Star TV, there wasn't much hand-wringing over it in the capital, New Delhi. Frankly, how did he matter? But a Murdoch-owned Star TV, to a government closeted for decades behind a protected economy, was a symbol of all the pernicious influences it wanted to keep out. It was a 'foreign' broadcaster, a 'cultural invader' owned by one of the most controversial media moguls in the world.

These tensions would culminate in a full-scale battle that would shape the Indian broadcast and media industry and relegate Star to failure for a long time. To contextualize the battles brewing between Star TV and the Indian government, between Murdoch and Chandra, between the whole idea of private and state broadcasting, we need to step back a bit.

The satellite invasion

If you are an Indian, chances are that you stopped watching DD, the state-controlled terrestrial TV network, a long time ago. Once upon a time, DD was all that Indians could view. Ever since its launch in 1959, it has shaped television broadcasting, simply by being there. Television sales and penetration really took off when India hosted the Asian Games in 1982 and colour transmission began. By the next year came *Show Theme*, arguably India's first sponsored programme, produced by TV personality Manju Singh.[1] Then, in 1984, a US-based non-governmental organization approached the Ministry of Information and Broadcasting to do a show with a message around family planning. India's biggest problem then was perceived to be extreme poverty coupled with a galloping population. The idea of a family planning message couched as entertainment had worked successfully in Catholic Mexico where overt messages were a strict no-no. The Indian government approved of the idea and India's first soap opera, *Hum Log*, featuring a typical lower-middle-class family facing everything—poverty, alcoholism and illiteracy—began airing in July 1984.

---

[1]   Whether *Show Theme* or *Hum Log* was the first sponsored programme on DD is a matter of debate.

It took off like a shot. Nanhe, Chutki and Badki became characters a whole generation of Indians can still recall clearly. More than 80 per cent of the 3.6 million Indian television sets at that time tuned in to *Hum Log* every week. (TV ratings did not as yet exist.) Its success spurred DD to look for more entertainment programming. *Buniyaad*, *Katha Sagar*, *Khandaan*, *Nukkad* and a host of other popular serials and sitcoms followed in the mid- to late-1980s. Telecast fees and commercial airtime rates on DD began rising.[2] From Rs 17 crore ($15 million) in 1983–84, DD's revenues rose to a reported Rs 210 crore ($120 million) in 1989–90.

Those were the golden days of DD. There was no competition except from cable operators who were showing pirated films in some large cities. However, DD's success bred corruption and complacency. There were whispers about the money that changed hands to get a show on-air. Still, nothing stopped either the growth in viewership or the long queue of producers that formed outside its headquarters every time a new show slot was up for bidding. India hit roughly 23 million TV homes by the turn of the decade. Though cable TV was growing, terrestrial broadcasting,[3] DD's domain, was safe because it was a government monopoly. DD's control over radio and television broadcasting was derived from the Indian Telegraph Act of 1885 where 'telegraph' was interpreted to cover the generation of signals for telecasting.

When CNN first burst on to the scene in 1991 on the back of the first Gulf War, there wasn't much concern in the government. It was seen as an elitist indulgence limited to a few top hotels in metros such as Bombay and Delhi. Then, later that year, Star TV with its four channels and, later, Zee TV came in. The Telegraph Act pre-dated cable and satellite broadcasting. Its definitions did not

---

[2]   Some parts in this section have been excerpted from my book, *The Indian Media Business*, fourth edition (New Delhi: Sage, 2013).

[3]   Terrestrial broadcasting involves relaying the signal by radio waves from the terrestrial or earth-based transmitter of a television station—DD has over 1400—to a TV home having an antenna.

cover those technologies and therefore there was nothing that could be done about them immediately. The signals from AsiaSat1 with its wide arc cutting across thirty-eight countries were unencrypted or open to access. They could be picked up by any cable operator who could then relay the signal through wires strung all over an urban landscape into homes. Zee TV (Hindi, October 1992) and Kalanithi Maran's Sun TV (Tamil, 1993), among others, jumped in and private broadcasting took off. The satellite invasion was well under way and DD started to feel the pinch.

When Basu, a soft-spoken, cerebral man with a reputation for efficiency, walked in as director general, DD had been without a chief for some time. 'In the previous five years a succession of director generals and ministers had changed, so DD was hardly doing anything to its programming. Also, it had acquired a bad reputation for corruption,' recalls Basu. A Central Bureau of Investigation inquiry was under way as well as litigation concerning the selection of shows in the past. Things were a mess. 'By chance I got a free hand—a genuinely free hand—to choose new shows,' says Basu. He chose *Shanti* and *Chandrakanta* among dozens of shows. *Shanti*, the first afternoon soap opera on Indian TV, became a rage. So did *Chandrakanta* and many of the others. Basu also set about wooing some of the biggest editors and journalists—Madhu Trehan, Karan Thapar and Vir Sanghvi—getting them on board to anchor shows on DD. Prannoy Roy, an economist, psephologist and journalist, was already on DD with *The World This Week*. By 1995, DD was rocking. Almost everyone at Star TV, Zee and Sun TV took note— not just of its success but also of the man behind it.

Then, several things happened.

First, in February 1995 came a Supreme Court ruling saying that airwaves were not the monopoly of the Indian government.[4] The judgement had its origins in the decision of the Cricket Association

---

4   Supreme Court of India: *The Secretary, Ministry of Information and Broadcasting v. Cricket Association of Bengal and ANR*. Date of judgement: 9 February 1995. Source: Indiakanoon.org.

of Bengal and the Board of Control for Cricket in India to sell the rights of the Hero Cup in 1994 to ESPN, a new private entrant into India. However, being a foreign broadcaster, ESPN was not allowed to uplink from within the country. This prevented it from broadcasting the match live from Calcutta. In a judgement on a suit filed by the Ministry of Information and Broadcasting against the Cricket Association of Bengal, the Supreme Court ruled that airwaves are public property and have to be used to foster plurality and diversity of views, opinions and ideas. This was implicit in Article 19(1) (a) of the Indian Constitution, granting the right of free speech to citizens, said the judgement. This gave courage to many private broadcasters and actually opened the floodgates. In light of the Supreme Court judgement, the Cable Television Networks (Regulation) Act was born in March 1995. It laid out the framework for setting up a cable TV operation in India. It also put a cap of 49 per cent on foreign equity in cable network companies. (That figure has since been raised to 100 per cent.)

Second, in July 1995 News Corp picked up the remaining 36.4 per cent in Star TV. It paid Hutchison Whampoa and Genza Investments (owned by Li personally) about $299 million. It also took over shareholder loans made by Genza and Hutchison to Star TV. That took the total price of Star TV to an estimated $870 million. For Li and his family, both rounds of Star TV's sale were hugely profitable. According to reports, Li personally made $350–400 million. This was the money he used to set up PCCW, now a large tech, telecom and media firm.

Third, Basu had been eying cricket for some time in order to drive up DD's viewership. In 1995, he bid for—and won—the rights to the cricket World Cup. However, for a variety of reasons, Basu had to go to court to fight for DD's right to broadcast the event. In January 1996, just two days before the final hearing, the-powers-that-be transferred Basu to the Department of Electronics as secretary. It was a promotion intended to get him out of DD.

'I was very disappointed and unhappy and decided to look for options,' says Basu. Even before he had settled into the Department of Electronics, job offers began to pour in. The first one was from Zee, the second from the Hinduja business family, which had just entered the cable business. However, Basu, a star CEO in Indian broadcasting by then, refused. In May 1996 he got a call from Gene Swinstead, managing director, Star TV India and Middle East, asking if he would meet Murdoch. He offered to fly him to any part of the world. 'I told him that I can't go rushing off without government approval. If Mr Murdoch wants to meet me he has to come to India,' remembers Basu. Within about five days, he got another call, this one from Murdoch himself. He was in Delhi and wanted to meet—should he drop by Basu's office or would Basu like to come to his hotel? Basu knew that if Murdoch walked into the Department of Electronics tongues wouldn't stop wagging, so he opted to go over to the presidential suite of the Grand Hyatt in Delhi.

A bureaucrat and a businessman

The first question Murdoch asked him was, 'What is your vision for broadcasting in India?' 'I told him that direct-to-home [DTH] is the future,' says Basu. And thus began a longish discussion on the merits of the technology and India's internecine cable wars. Since there was no licensing, any cable operator could undercut and take away consumers from a rival in an area. This sometimes led to violent clashes, with the underworld being called in to settle disputes in some parts of Bombay.

At DD, Basu had looked seriously at DTH as a way to sidestep the mess of cable and reach more people. Basu felt that DTH, which uses the Ku-band for transmission, was a more 'economical technology'. Its signals could be picked up by individual homes, which would buy a set-top box and a small dish to receive signals, instead of going through cable operators. This would make the business direct-to-consumer and offer broadcasters better control over both distribution and subscription revenues. The next chapter deals in more detail with the merits of DTH versus cable when we tackle the time Basu actually tried to launch it in India. But for now, remember, this was 1996; Indians had just begun to accept satellite TV through a cable operator. The idea of broadcasting directly into homes was mind-boggling.

The funny part was, 'Murdoch listened [and talked] but kept going in and out of the room to make calls.'[5] At one point he asked Basu what DTH would cost. 'My estimate was $500 million,' says Basu. After about four hours, Murdoch said, 'Mr Basu, $500 million has been transferred to the Star account in Mumbai and we have booked [seven transponders] on PanAmSat's PAS4. Would you join me?'

Basu was startled by the speed of Murdoch's decision-making. It was a quality that would keep surprising him over the years he worked for Murdoch. Basu knew he could get into trouble for joining a foreign broadcaster so he asked for time to think. He met with I.K. Gujral, then minister for external affairs, and sounded him out. 'I asked him, "How would the government react if I took a job with Murdoch?" Gujral replied, "The government will be proud [since one of its officers was being picked for a good job]",' says Basu. This was in June 1996. On 1 October, after serving a three-month notice period, Basu became the first CEO of News Television India.

This was the first senior appointment Star TV had made from within India—the lesson from Channel [V] was well learnt. 'Before Basu, it was the Wild West, people were coming and going—Gene Swinstead, Andrew Carnegie . . . Basu was brought in to get DTH going, manage relations with the [Indian] government, give Star an Indian face and run the business,' reckons Sameer Nair, who was then a producer-director for interstitials for Star Movies. These are pieces of content—say an interview or a piece of trivia—that fill the breaks during a film. Gary Davey, then CEO for Star TV Asia, says,

---

[5] The details on the Basu–Murdoch interaction are based on Rathikant Basu's version of events since Rupert Murdoch did not respond to my request for an interview.

'I chose Rathikant Basu. I got to know him in his role at DD; he was clever and competitive. DD was such a big, complex bureaucracy to handle but he made for a formidable competitor. I recommended him to Rupert . . . he has an amazing instinct for big opportunities. Once he [Rupert] makes a decision to do something, he is persistent and patient. The prize is usually worth it.'

That was not strictly true this time round.

Some good news

Prannoy Roy was on his way to becoming a household name. An economist and an accountant by training, Roy introduced the idea of psephology to India. Elections fascinated him (they still do), and the electoral system in the world's largest democracy is where his combination of skills was best used. NDTV, a firm he set up with his wife Radhika Roy, produced its first show, a weekly global news round-up, *The World This Week*, on DD in 1988. Roy anchored it. Then NDTV was asked to do election analysis for DD, the only time DD allowed live coverage of anything from a private producer. It was a peculiar situation. Unlike many developing countries, the press in India was (and is) free. But electronic news was still the preserve of the state and 'live' domestic news from a private producer/broadcaster was a big no-no.

In February 1995, just a few days before the Supreme Court's judgement that 'airwaves are not a monopoly of the Indian government', NDTV began airing the first private news bulletin on DD, thanks to Basu, who was then heading DD. Over the years, Roy and his team did shows such as *News Tonight*, *The News Hour* and *Good Morning India* on DD, still India's largest broadcaster. This helped foster the growth of a robust private news broadcast business. Sadly, DD never got the autonomy that would have allowed it to make news or entertainment shows the way an autonomous public service broadcaster such as BBC does. It did not have the most critical tool needed to become a credible alternative—independence. Its purse strings and administration were (still are) controlled by the central government.[6] As private broadcasting grew, producers such as NDTV, TV18, UTV and others walked in to fill the vacuum that the lack of a competitive, high-quality public news broadcaster created.

When Basu shifted to Star TV in October 1996, the first thing he did was ask Roy to do a news show for Star Plus. Roy agreed and *Star News*, an English news bulletin, began airing at 9 p.m. Because regulation forbade live news, most private news producers delayed their broadcasts. NDTV, for instance, would send the news to Hong Kong at 8.50 p.m., but it would be telecast only at 9 p.m. 'It was news that made us take off—that along with Channel [V] and Star Movies. That was the first time we saw success among the chattering classes. News was getting in more money than Channel [V],' remembers John O'Loan, the man who had set up Sky News. He was pulled in to help with news programming in India.[7] At one point, more than a third of Star's revenues in India came from that one news show.[8] Later, a Hindi bulletin, *Star Samachar*, was launched with Vinod Dua, Mrinal Pandey and other popular Hindi anchors. However, it didn't take off quite the way the English version had. Incidentally, when he started doing a show for Star, DD pulled Roy's shows off the national channel.

---

[6] Technically, DD has been part of the autonomous Prasar Bharati Corporation since 1997. However, it cannot hire or fire people and its budgets are controlled by the central government.

[7] John O'Loan launched Sky News in the UK and has since worked on thirty television projects across the world with a speciality in news. He was in charge of helping Star set up news operations, first as a one-off show, then a twenty-four-hour channel in 1998. He is currently a non-executive independent director on the NDTV India board.

[8] Though News Corp was (and is) listed, getting the numbers for the Asia and India businesses was a challenge, especially for the years prior to 2010. So the Star India and Asia revenue numbers were culled from old interviews and estimates among other sources. They may not be correct to the last decimal, but I hope they are roughly in the right range. The post-2010 numbers have been put together by Singapore-based Media Partners Asia.

Next came the 'Hindi dubs', courtesy of the Aussies and Britons sitting in Hong Kong, say insiders from that time. All the Star Plus English shows such as *Baywatch, The Simpsons* and *The Bold and the Beautiful* were dubbed in Hindi. Dubs might have worked in another market. But in India, with its robust local content industry, local dubs were a huge flop. 'Star TV became the laughing stock of the media,' says a Star employee of that time. 'Advertisers were confused: should Star Plus be compared to Zee TV for ratings and rates?'

Then, a slew of shows, many in Hindi, shifted from DD to Star Plus—*Chandrakanta, Tu Tu Main Main* and *The Priya Tendulkar Show* among them. This was possible because DD operated on a telecast fee model—it simply sold slots of time to producers and made money on the fee they paid. The intellectual property rights or IPR of the show vested with the producer, unlike in private broadcasting where shows were (and are) commissioned and all rights belonged to the broadcaster. Star also commissioned shows such as Neena Gupta's *Saans* (1998), the story of a woman who has to rebuild her life after her husband walks out of their marriage. It drew critical acclaim and audiences, becoming one of the few Star programmes to land in the top twenty shows. (INTAM, a service from research agency ORG-MARG, had begun tracking TV viewing by then.)

Basu also started to hire senior people from DD—Indira Mansingh as head of news, Bimla Bhalla as executive director, Urmila Gupta as head of the DTH project under ISkyB, V. Basavaraj and Saroj Chandola in programming, among others.

Most of these moves had negative repercussions. Taking shows and people away from DD caused enormous bad blood with the Indian government, and getting into Hindi programming soured things with Subhash Chandra. His agreement with Star meant that Hindi was his territory.

If by buying Star Murdoch had bought himself a head start of at least a year or two over competitors, then what followed after Basu's coming in actually set it back pretty badly.

5

Star Speaks in Hindi

A rival called Subhash Chandra, a technology called DTH and a government on the warpath

The partnership between Star and Zee worked until Rathikant Basu came along, believes Subhash Chandra, and then started going downhill. Zee's shareholders' agreement with News Corp stated that Indian languages were Zee's territory, and here was Star launching Hindi shows. Basu contends, 'The legal advice we got was that as long as we didn't cross 50 per cent [of the total programming in Hindi] it was fine.' Chandra doesn't agree: 'Basu misinterpreted the shareholders' agreement and probably misled News Corp as to how much Hindi programming was allowed. Our deal was clear; Zee would handle all Hindi channels and programming and Star would focus on English shows and channels. Neither would venture into the other's market.'

For Star, the agreement meant it was operating in a booming market with its hands tied firmly behind its back. It was a position

Chandra probably wanted News Corp to remain in. Zee Telefilms was the biggest player with Rs 123 crore ($35 million) in revenues in the year ending March 1996. 'Zee was taking them [Star] for a ride. It was in Zee's interest to keep them in English,' says one senior consultant who has worked for both firms.

However, given the shape of the market and Murdoch's characteristic ambition and aggression it would have been impossible to stop Star for long. By 1995, Sony Entertainment Television (a part of Columbia TriStar) came into being in a joint venture with Indian partners and rapidly gained popularity. Home TV (from The Hindustan Times Limited, the holding company for what is known as HT Media now) and Eenadu (from Ramoji Rao) were some of the other channels that were launched.

When Basu moved to Star in October 1996, 18 million of India's 57 million homes were cable- and satellite-enabled—up from 1.2 million out of 35 million just four years earlier. The total revenue (advertising and subscription) of the TV business had grown over eightfold from Rs 496 crore ($192 million) in 1992 to Rs 4100 crore ($1.1 billion) in 1996. More than half of this was money that consumers paid as their cable bill. Star (India) was doing all right with its English image and premium ad rates but was still a small player in News Corp's scheme of things. Star TV was losing close to $80 million on its Asia operations every year.

'The primary reason Sony succeeded was because the territory had been left virgin by Star. Zee was already doing well with *Tara* and other shows. Star imported DD [by hiring Basu] while Sony did programming that Star should have done,' says Raghav Bahl, founder of TV18. Private broadcasting was taking its first giant strides in Hindi, Tamil, Telugu and other languages, but Star, which was one of the first entrants in 1991, couldn't join the party. It began to strain at the leash.

Bruce Churchill, who was then deputy CEO at Star TV Asia, sums it up thus: 'We figured we couldn't be a force until we did Hindi and other Indian languages. Zee was very successful, but we were prevented from doing Hindi. Because of Chandra we couldn't make changes in the agreement to take advantage of the growth potential. Gary [Davey, CEO Star TV Asia] and I started to look at whether we could get out of the joint venture. We started doing Hindi programming, the language of TV. The agreement was ambiguous. It said X hours of programming, not when. Chandra started getting antsy.'

Davey adds that 'the expectations of the two parties were never properly shaped. Chandra's was that Sky would never do local content; that was never our understanding. There were complex clauses in the original agreement on what Sky could and could not do; it was open to interpretation. Everybody who read it had his own idea of what it meant.' This led to sniping, letters and the expected friction in such a situation. 'When Chandra started protesting we slowed down and that is when discussion about the merger [between Star and Zee] began,' says Basu.

But we are getting ahead of the story. Let's rewind a bit.

'When Basu came, it shifted the centre of power from Hong Kong to India,' remembers Raj Nayak, then a senior member of the ad sales team. Basu (or Rodney, as he was code-named by the Mumbai team) also brought with him the bureaucracy and thinking of a government organization, known locally as the sarkari touch, say several people from that time. Speak to anyone from the first team and the impression is of a collegiate, informal place where people called each by their first names, were paid well, worked and partied hard. By all accounts News Television India was a happy place even if it did not get an audience or revenues as big as DD.

'Basu's coming brought two different operating cultures. The informal place was changing into a bureaucratic one with the proverbial red light outside the door. Everything needed several people to sign off which meant that approvals took ages. They [the new team hired by Basu] came late to work and went off early. And everything was compared, office sizes, meal trays, perks, everything. An Us versus Them culture crept in,' says one senior member of the old team. 'Basu was an intelligent man but his team was a bunch of paper-pushing bureaucrats, except for Bimla Bhalla and Indira Mansingh. One of them used to move around with a spittoon,' says an executive with a laugh. Basu reckons that all he did was enforce rules, which may have seemed bureaucratic to a team that had been left largely to its own devices.

To this atmosphere of internal conflict, add several external battles.

An angry government, a hostile press

Chandra has always portrayed himself—and is seen as—a 'nationalistic' businessman. His relationship with the Congress party and the Rashtriya Swayamsevak Sangh, the ideological parent of the Bharatiya Janata Party, are well documented in his book and elsewhere. Luckily for him, in the India of 1996–97 the anti-foreign feeling was pretty strong. The country had just opened its economy to 'foreign investment'—the very term was viewed with excitement and a lot of suspicion in my growing-up years in the 1980s and 1990s.

Then the Nikki Bedi incident happened. In May 1995, a gay activist, Ashok Row Kavi, called Mahatma Gandhi a 'bastard bania' on Bedi's somewhat racy chat show, *Nikki Tonight*, on Star TV. Tushar Gandhi, the Mahatama's grandson, happened to be watching and was incensed; so were the press and the government. It was the sort of insensitive thing people expected a 'foreign channel' to do. Gandhi slapped a Rs 50 crore lawsuit (over $14 million then) against Star TV, TV18 (the producers), Bedi and Kavi. Though Star TV apologized, pulled the show off-air and made all the right noises, the incident added fuel to the xenophobic fire and coloured regulators' perception of the firm for years.

As a senior Star TV insider from that time says, 'Zee was Indian and well connected; Star was not Indian and poorly connected. Star was foreign with a capital F. It was not just some nondescript foreign firm but one owned by Rupert Murdoch, hated and feared in equal measure. Nobody knew Richard Li, but Rupert bothered local media proprietors and government officials.' The press was feeding this 'anti-foreign, Murdoch-is-destroying-India's-culture kind of feeling. The print media,' says the insider, 'was terrified of Rupert.' There was apprehension that he might just try to enter the print business.

At that time, Murdoch was still known more for his newspapers such as the *Sun* and the *Times* than for his channels such as Sky TV and Fox. Other foreign players such as Sony, Turner International, Viacom and Disney did not have to face the bias that comes from being 'foreign' for three reasons. One, they didn't have a presence in print. Two, they weren't identified with news. And three, none had a clearly recognizable face à la Murdoch. None got the negative press that Star received, almost on a regular basis.

It was while these things were going on—the sniping between Chandra and Star over Hindi, a hostile press, deep resentment against the foreign cultural invader—that Basu hired some senior people from DD over 1996 and 1997.

This was the proverbial red flag. 'All the forces that Basu had offended worked against DTH [which Basu would attempt soon]; internally too the team didn't support him,' says one insider from Basu's team. Basu's fat salary cheque, black Mercedes and upmarket Nepean Sea Road flat in Bombay had already caused 'deep resentment among the IAS babus against him,' reckons Bahl. Basu relives those days. 'I became the object of everyone's envy and anger. Everybody—the government and the other private channels which didn't want me to join Star—was after my blood. Every two days there were negative stories in the newspapers about me.'

It was against this backdrop of internal and external conflict that Star was attempting to make its biggest investment in India—in a new broadcasting technology called DTH.

The DTH ban

Currently, India has five distinct technologies offering TV signals: terrestrial (DD), DTH (Tata Sky, DishTV), online services (Netflix, Amazon Prime Video), IPTV or Internet protocol TV, which Airtel offers and Jio will soon, and cable and satellite (Star, Sony, Zee). The last decade or so alone has seen the rise of both DTH and online services.

But in 1997 there was only DD and what we called cable and satellite TV. In most developed countries, however, cable TV developed on the back of terrestrial television, which was delivered via cable. In India, terrestrial was always the preserve of the government. Satellite broadcasting is what rode on the cable wires that operators had strung up to offer pirated films in the 1980s. Therefore, 'cable' and 'satellite' are synonymous in our heads. Satellite TV, the way Murdoch saw it, was completely different—he was thinking of DTH or Ku-band transmission. The C-band transponders from which Star was broadcasting had a wide arc covering thirty-eight countries and anybody within those countries could catch the signal. For the most part, these were cable operators or large firms that could invest in the 2 to 3 metre dishes and other equipment needed to capture and relay the signal.

However, a new technology called DTH or direct-to-home, which used Ku-band, had emerged. It was a more focused signal that could be sold directly to consumers who could pick it up with dishes of less than a metre. A home that signed on had to buy a dish and a set-top box. It is the technology that had almost bankrupted News Corp when it invested in it in the late 1980s. But BSkyB, the entity that emerged from the whole process, was by now profitable. (See Chapter 2, 'Rupert's Discovery of Asia'.) It is a technology Murdoch has championed across the world since then. Sky Italia and Sky Deutschland were set up or acquired by News Corp, making it one of the largest satellite TV operators in the world at one point.[1]

DTH offered two distinct advantages, especially for India.

One, violent disputes on the ground over cable territories were common in the 1990s. Given how vicious things were, DTH was a great way of sidestepping the whole cable route and going direct to consumer. This would also mean control over pay revenues. Most

---

[1]   Sky was acquired by Comcast in 2018.

channels in India were unencrypted then and there was no concept of pay revenues. Cable operators kept all the money that subscribers paid; broadcasters got nothing. It has changed a bit but not much. In 2018, about 25 per cent of what was collected from India's 197 million TV homes went back to broadcasters—the bulk of this was from DTH operators. Cable still remains fairly opaque.

Two, in a huge, heterogeneous market like India, the investment in wiring up the whole country with cable would have been prohibitive. DTH offered a great option to distribute and monetize TV signals.

ISkyB, News Corp's DTH service, was in an advanced stage of readiness by the beginning of 1997. It had a $27-million-a-year deal with PanAmSat's PAS4 for seven transponders for the Indian market. The price of the DTH kit (the set-top box and dish that a subscriber would need) being discussed was Rs 12,000 ($342) a year and a monthly subscription of between Rs 399 and Rs 500 ($11–14) for a forty-channel bouquet. This would include Star TV, south Indian language channels from Sun TV, DD and other Hindi channels. The target was to reach 5,00,000 subscribers by year three and break even within three to five years. ISkyB was scheduled to launch on 2 April 1997, pending government permission. The excitement in News Corp was high—the company would finally have a local distribution business and a direct connect with viewers. This was the big business that Murdoch expected Basu to deliver on.

Towards the end of March 1997 Basu was to hold a press conference to demonstrate the ISkyB service. More than thirty foreign journalists were flying in for the demonstration, which was meant to herald a new broadcasting technology in India. A slew of full-page ads announcing the demonstration, however, raised regulatory hackles—there was a sense that News Corp was trying to illegally introduce DTH to India. Just a day before the demo, the minister for information and broadcasting, C.M. Ibrahim, held a press conference saying that there was no question of DTH services being allowed until the broadcasting bill was passed. To save face, the demonstration was done using a C-band transponder. The Star teams in Hong Kong, New York and India flew into damage control mode, holding back press releases and recalling embargoed ones.

The thirty-page bill was introduced on 16 May 1997 to bring much-needed order to India's broadcasting industry, regulated so far by the Telegraph Act of 1885. Ideally, the purpose should have been to provide a regulatory framework for the private broadcasting industry, which by then consisted of over fifty channels. This would have facilitated its growth and ensured that it contributed to employment and tax generation. However, intense lobbying by domestic firms turned it into an Indian versus foreign or a DD versus private broadcasters slanging match.

Soon after, on 16 July, the government issued a notification banning DTH until the broadcasting bill was enacted into law. Many of the press clippings from that time are full of conspiracy theories. The swadeshi lobby, the broadcasters, the bureaucrats—everybody was fighting with everybody else. The bill, it had begun to seem, was simply a way to stall Star's DTH project. While several firms were impacted—Indonesia's Shinawatra and Modi Entertainment, among others—the hardest hit was News Corp's ISkyB. It had a transponder deal in place and about 185 employees—with all the accompanying overheads—in India.

'Through the Siticable joint venture [that Star had signed with Zee's cable arm in 1994] we became aware of how limited and difficult it was to roll out a decent quality cable network across the country. That's how we came to the conclusion that the Ku-band is an opportunity. We started the licence process and took the Ku-band on PanAmSat4. We had a difficult time getting the licence. Then the Ku-band was banned. PanAmSat had an early mover advantage. All of those who wanted to enter the business worked at delaying our permission. Our competition was more politically influential than we were,' says David Haslingden, who was heading Fox International Channels then.

This shadow-boxing between Star and Zee, private and public broadcasting, foreign and Indian, ended up harming the regulatory framework of Indian broadcasting for good. India still doesn't have a broadcasting bill or any comprehensive, big-picture facilitative framework for the industry. 'Thanks to the government's ludicrous obsession with DTH, much of the debate on this bill is becoming a referendum on this technology. It happens to be the clause of least relevance to the vast majority of viewers,' said media expert Sevanti Ninan then.[2]

Most analysts reckon that Star TV would have been profitable much earlier if it hadn't made the DTH foray. 'Having launched satellite TV in the UK we knew it was a fantastic opportunity. But complex regulatory issues plus a high degree of paranoia in the Indian press which actively opposed it meant we were unable to launch DTH,' sums up Davey.

Even after the policy fog cleared in 2000, Star got a licence to launch DTH only in 2005, almost a decade after it had first started investing in it. By then Zee had launched (in 2003) and established its service. (For more on DTH, read Chapter 8, 'Star-crossed'.)

The beginning of the end

Meanwhile, back in 1997, the Department of Personnel and Training, Government of India, sent Basu a notice asking him to resign from his job at Star. It said he had violated the service rules that prohibited government employees from accepting a job within two years of retirement. Basu and his lawyers argued that the rules allowed for it as long as he was not a pensioner—which he wasn't. Though he had retired, Basu had not applied for a pension. News Television India, too, got a letter asking it to sack Basu within fifteen days. There was even talk of an inquiry by the Central Bureau of Investigation. Essentially, the government had got its knife into Basu. Finally, according to Basu, it was his chat with the then prime minister, I.K. Gujral, that led the bureaucracy to call off its hounds.

By then the damage had been done. The DTH project was in limbo. However, speculation in the Asian trade and business press

---

[2]   *Cable and Satellite Magazine*, September–October 1997.

continued to suggest that the official clearance was just round the corner. For many months, the weekly Monday morning meetings with Hong Kong began with a discussion on the status of the permission. Many within the system, especially the Mumbai gang, which was at loggerheads with Basu's style of functioning, saw this as his failure to do the one big job he had been hired for—gain the government's support.

News Corp, however, has a remarkably federal structure—CEOs are left free to do their own thing. 'In News Corp nobody ever got fired for making a mistake, they got fired for not doing anything,' explains O'Loan. To his credit, Basu immediately came up with something else. 'DTH was getting into problems, so the only way to counter Chandra and get some clout for Star was to launch a news channel,' says Basu.

That is how Star News, India's first private news channel, was born in 1998.

Prannoy to the rescue

Indira Mansingh did her master's in English literature from the University of Allahabad and later specialized in communications studies from George Washington University in the US. During Basu's time she was the deputy director general in charge of clearing all current affairs shows on DD. 'I always wanted to do a twenty-four-hour news channel because I had lived and studied in the US. You can watch news at your choice of time. Plus the economics of a twenty-four-hour news channel are much better because you can repeat so much. Basu and I had talked about it at DD,' she remembers. When Basu shifted to Star, Mansingh joined too as head of news.

'The [Star News] bulletins were wildly successful. Those were heady days because all the freedom we had looked for [at DD] was available,' says she. Since the news show was programmed by NDTV there was not much she could do editorially. Prannoy Roy didn't allow much intervention but Mansingh kept an eye on what was going on-air. Basu's diktat was "'I don't want the Star News bulletin off-air", so we had to be careful. Prannoy and I never agreed. If it was a political story I would deal with Radhika and she would agree to requests for balance, but Prannoy wouldn't give an inch,' remembers Mansingh.

When Mansingh joined Star TV she got talking to Basu about a twenty-four-hour news channel again. Basu, who liked the idea, spoke to Roy and Hong Kong about it. General elections were due in 1998. They are the biggest political event in India, the world's largest democracy. However, at the time, except for DD and the newspapers, nobody covered them. Since news was the most popular bit of programming on Star Plus, why not launch a news channel, thought Basu. He called up Murdoch and said that he had a project in mind, a news channel. 'Murdoch asked what costs I was looking at. About $10 million a year, $50 million over five years, I replied. His response [was], "For that amount you don't have to ask me, go ahead,"' says Basu. That is how a unique deal was worked out between News Television India and NDTV.

News Television would finance a twenty-four-hour news channel, giving it support and infrastructure. NDTV would produce the channel and have complete editorial control. NDTV got an advance to buy the equipment plus a fixed fee, which began at $10 million with a built-in 15 per cent escalation clause, total editorial control and all copyrights. Star would monetize the channel and keep all the profit. It was a sweetheart deal for NDTV. Star paid for everything that NDTV built its reputation on while Star had no control over the content.

That is how, in August 1997, Dilshad Master-Kumar, who was heading operations for Star out of Mumbai, was moved to Delhi. Her job was to help launch a news channel—she would report to Mansingh and operate out of the NDTV office acting as the Star TV representative. When she walked into the NDTV office on day one, John O'Loan, the man who had set up Sky News, was up in the studio fixing the news desk. He asked her to pass him the pliers, finished what he was doing and introduced himself.

To Master-Kumar, this captured the 'roll up your sleeves and do the job' attitude Star and NDTV had in those days. News Corp rolled out training, knowledge and equipment for Star News from all over the globe. There was a whole team from Hong Kong helping with graphics and promos. 'Rupert is like that. If he gets excited about an idea he sends his best people,' says Basu. That, incidentally, is true for all the businesses News Corp got into later—DTH, radio, outdoor.

Star News was inaugurated in February 1998 by Prime Minister Gujral. It was a huge success. Roy and his team at NDTV did a good job, supported by News Corp's global system. Murdoch knew the space—Sky News and Fox News were behind him. But the biggest reason for its success was the hunger in Indians for news about their own country. It was the first time that this chatty, chaotic, argumentative democracy had a sense of participating in what was happening in the country. Today, when we have the Internet, an omnipresent social media and about 400 news channels, it is hard to imagine the impact that the first twenty-four-hour independent news channel had. The country had just begun opening up and was trying to figure out its place in the world. And NDTV gave us a window into India and the rest of the world. What is more, it invited us to participate in discussions on issues that mattered—unlike the newspapers, which just stated the news. In the valuation exercise being done for the merger with Zee later that year, 'Star News had a $100 million valuation and we had spent just $10 million,' says Basu. The figure, according to Basu, was about a fourth of the overall valuation for News Television.

The merger, which never happened, was nevertheless an important twist in the Indian broadcasting story.

When Star and Zee almost merged

Star's forays into Hindi programming had been annoying Zee. The friction between the two firms in the market, in the corridors of power and otherwise, was intense. The failure of Star's most ambitious project in India, DTH, and its inability to expand had all built up tension between the two rivals. That was when Basu came up with the idea of a merger in mid-1998.

'Zee TV acquired content from Zee Telefilms [the listed entity]. 50 per cent of the programming cost was paid by Star since it was a partner in the uplink firm Asia Today Limited. The 50:50 partnership was bearing 100 per cent of the cost of programming. I suggested a merger so that costs and revenues could be on a merged basis, both companies could benefit enormously,' says Basu. In March 1998 Zee was Rs 173 crore ($47 million) in revenues and profitable. At some point in mid-1998 Basu met Chandra in Hong Kong and floated the idea of a merger between Star and Zee. Chandra agreed and the two of them travelled to London to meet Murdoch.

Basu went in first to meet Murdoch on his own: 'I gave him a copy of the presentation and before I could reach page three he shut the booklet, banged it on the table and said, "For the first time some sense is coming out of India. How do we go ahead?" I told him Chandra was downstairs and he said, "Let's do it today."' Chandra, however, wanted an independent valuation. Basu recalls that Murdoch tried to persuade Chandra against it because it would have prolonged the discussion. He was willing to throw in a generous cash component along with a 50 per cent shareholding and the first chairmanship. Chandra wouldn't budge. Soon, the independent valuation exercise began and things started to go wrong. There are two very different versions of what happened—one from Basu and the other from Chandra. The outcome, in any case, was that the merger, which could have led the Indian broadcasting industry in another direction, did not happen. 'Murdoch terminated all negotiations and sent me a note saying, "Go all out and compete with them." And we did,' says Basu.

Star started commissioning Hindi shows such as *Kora Kagaz* and *Saans*. 'That is when [the] relationship broke. It was the final straw,' says Dilshad Master-Kumar, who headed operations for Star Plus and later for Star News. Later in August 1999, Zee Telefilms filed a suit in the London High Court to stop Star Plus from airing Hindi programming. Soon after, the two divorced and *Kaun Banega Crorepati* was born. More on that in the next chapter.

Murdoch makes changes

'Star News was a big feather in Rodney's cap,' says a Star insider from the time. The implication being it was the only one. There are a variety of opinions about what Basu's tenure did for Star. 'DTH failed but what he did with News and Plus is important,' contends Mansingh.

She is right. In hindsight it is easy to see what worked and what failed. While the introduction of Hindi did declare Star's intent, it fell far short of the audience levels of both Zee and Sony. DTH was in limbo and Star News was a relatively small project. Zee had already touched Rs 226 crore ($54 million) in revenues by March 1999, seven years after its launch. And it dominated the ratings charts. In March 1999 only one show from Star, *Saans*, even made it to the top twenty. Star Plus's top line was estimated at only $20 million to $30 million (Rs 80 crore to Rs 130 crore) though it had entered the market earlier. In fiscal 1999 News Television made close to $100 million (Rs 428 crore), largely because of pay revenues, sports, the integration of Channel [V] into the firm and Star News among its other revenues streams. 'I don't think I had a great contribution to make but I learnt a lot. Working with Rupert Murdoch was a great experience; you don't get that kind of freedom even in the private sector,' says Basu when asked how he reviews his days at Star.

As the weeks turned into months and the DTH permission remained elusive, Star was left wondering how to best use its team. Some got frustrated and left. Others were put to work on pointless projects—market research, field trips to map locations best suited for an uplink station, that sort of thing. And in the background played the endless loop of hope that the permission to launch DTH would come soon. On the other hand, newspapers began to speculate on how soon heads would roll.

The feeling of impending doom was building up. Something had to give.

On a Sunday evening in March 1999 Murdoch met with Davey in Hong Kong. They agreed that things had come to a head in India and the time had come for a change in management. They were tired of waiting and frustrated by the lack of scale in the business. After the meeting, Davey called Peter Mukerjea. He told Mukerjea that they had decided to appoint him CEO. Would he accept? 'Is the pope Catholic?' asked a delighted Mukerjea rhetorically. He had been waiting for just such an opportunity after six years of doing a good job at ad sales. 'I went out and had a serious drink with a couple of friends. It had all happened very suddenly; it wasn't a plan that I was party to,' Mukerjea confessed to me a year later.[3] But two years of Basu's five-year contract still remained. How could a change of guard take place?

This one, say people from that time, was a lesson in how to handle senior managers when you wanted to say bye-bye politely. In March 1999 Star TV split its India operations into three parts— entertainment would be headed by CEO Peter Mukerjea, while news and current affairs and DTH would be headed by executive chairman Rathikant Basu. In typical News Corp fashion, Davey and company did not waste any time. The senior managers from Hong Kong came down to India and parked themselves at the Leela Kempinski hotel, close to Star's office at Masterpiece in Andheri (east) in Mumbai. Mukerjea met the top team at the Leela in the presence of Basu and was informed about the change formally. There would be a transition period of a few weeks. (Ironically, Mukerjea would be dealt with in exactly the same manner in 2006.)

The story of Basu being sidelined is the Mumbai team's and the media's version of events. According to Basu himself, having

---

[3]   Peter Mukerjea is currently in jail. He has been quoted from several extensive interviews I had with him between 2000 and 2006 as a media editor for ABP's *Businessworld* magazine. Much of the background material on how he was thinking also comes from the transcripts of those interviews.

failed to realize his DTH dream, the continuous struggle against the government had got to him. He says he told Murdoch that he wanted to leave. When Murdoch asked him what he proposed to do next he said he had a clutch of regional channels in mind. Murdoch agreed to let him go on three conditions. One, Murdoch took a 5 per cent stake (for $1 million) in Basu's new venture, Broadcast Worldwide, with an option to take it up to 20 per cent.[4] Two, Basu would continue to be on the payroll of Star and draw his salary and perks until the end of his five-year contract in 2001. Three, he would not launch a Hindi or English channel for the next two years.

The truth of what happened probably lies somewhere in between. Basu had achieved what he could at Star, the government was hostile to the company and Basu's presence was only making the situation worse.

Soon after, in April, AsiaSat1 was replaced by AsiaSat3S. This allowed Star to go digital. Three months later, in August 1999, Star TV dropped its DTH plans and pulled out of its seven-transponder deal with PanAmSat on PAS4. In the financial year 1999 it wrote off $33 million on the ISkyB project. In the same month Zee Telefilms filed a suit in the London High Court to stop Star Plus from airing Hindi-language programming. An acrimonious divorce ensued where Zee bought out Star's holding in Zee and Siticable. Chandra paid out just over $296 million, going by Zee's March 2000 annual report.

By this time, Channel [V] had slowed down. MTV India and other music channels were giving it intense competition.

After nine years in India, Star had a news channel it did not programme, a sports channel in a joint venture (ESPN-Star Sports) and an entertainment channel that was a distant No. 3 to Zee and Sony. After sinking in millions of dollars it didn't have a DTH business or any distribution assets in one of the fastest-growing TV

---

[4] Rathikant Basu's new firm launched Tara Bangla and other regional channels in 2000.

markets in the world. And what was most galling was that this was after having been one of the first to enter the market.

But Murdoch wasn't done with India. He'd just wiped the slate clean. Star was ready to start all over again.

Part IV

Peter Mukerjea (1999–2007)

6

The Sixty Minutes That Saved Star

James Murdoch, Amitabh Bachchan, Ekta Kapoor and an unbeatable combination

'What's that stuff he's selling?' asked James Murdoch, pointing to a *gajrewala* at the window of the car we were travelling in. The tiny white garlands of jasmine flowers were beautiful. The gajrewala looked on expectantly as I explained that the garland is used to decorate one's hair. 'I don't have enough hair,' he said with a laugh, touching his head.[1]

At twenty-seven, James Murdoch was guileless and full of beans. He had the enthusiasm and curiosity of an intelligent, restless mind and the irreverence of a teenager. Like most Harvard dropouts, he

---

[1] Most of this chapter is based on notes from my interactions with James Murdoch in 2000 in Mumbai and in 2002 in Hong Kong. The 21st Century Fox team did not respond to my request for an interview.

had done several things. He had set up his own music company (Rawkus Records), which specialized in rap metal bands, and then sold it. He had created a cartoon strip, Albrecht the Hun, about a Hun who preferred literary pursuits. When he finally got around to joining News Corp, he chose to figure out the Internet as the head of new media strategy. He bought several businesses across China and India at the peak of the dotcom boom—an exercise that had News Corp writing off $300 million worth of investments later. In December 1999, dad Rupert Murdoch asked him to 'think about China'.

In the summer of 2000, on his first visit to India as chairman of the Star Group (the Asia business), I had a wonderfully frank interview with him at the company office in Andheri, in the northern suburbs of Mumbai.[2] After the interview, Peter Mukerjea, CEO, News Television, and James were on their way to south Mumbai for a meeting. Since my office in Worli was on their way, Mukerjea offered to drop me off and we got chatting about gajrewalas and other things. James was like a kid who couldn't get over all that was happening on the streets of Mumbai while Mukerjea was excited about an upcoming show, *Kaun Banega Crorepati*. 'We have got Amitabh Bachchan to host it,' he said in that lisping British accent that I came to associate with him over the next few years. He turned around in the front seat while sharing the news. I smiled politely.

This was April 2000. India had about 100 entertainment channels, the first multiplexes were opening up, and we had tasted both the Internet and private FM radio. Dozens of new shows were being launched every week, so another new one was not exactly headline-grabbing news, even if the 'Big B'—as Amitabh Bachchan was popularly known—was hosting it. Mukerjea had been CEO for a year, but Star remained a laggard. India had done well, bringing in a nice chunk of the $111 million in Asia revenues in the financial

---

[2]   The interview was done along with my (then) senior colleague Niranjan Rajadhyaksha. We were both working for ABP's *Businessworld* magazine. The magazine is now owned by Anurag Batra.

year ending June 1999. Much of this was thanks to increased ad revenues from Star News, the integration of Channel [V] into Star TV and the encryption of channels such as Star Movies. Encryption meant that a trickle of pay revenues had started coming in. However, overall, the satellite television business in Asia continued to bleed—$141 million that year. About a fifth of those losses came from Star's disastrous DTH foray. According to estimates, News Corp had by then lost over $1.5 billion in Asia—primarily in India and China. The whole Asian satellite TV business brought in just about 8 per cent of News Corp's top line. Star was far from being out of the woods.[3]

~

Soon after that interview, I went off to Cambridge on a fellowship. When I returned four months later in August 2000, Star was not just out of the woods, it was the king of the jungle. Most of India's 33 million cable TV homes stopped everything to watch *Kaun Banega Crorepati* at 9 p.m. on Star Plus every night from Monday to Thursday. On the back of the licensed version of *Who Wants to Be a Millionaire* and two daily soaps, it had become the largest, most popular channel by far. And News Corp was on a renewed investment spree in India with the almost $300 million that Subhash Chandra had paid it for the divorce. It was expanding into radio, had made over $100 million worth of investments in Internet start-ups in India, had invested in a cable company, was producing shows with BBC, and was planning a health channel among a host of other things. News Television was the hottest

---

[3] Though News Corp was (and is) listed, getting the numbers for the Asia and India businesses was a challenge, especially for the years prior to 2010. So they were culled from old interviews and estimates among other sources. They may not be correct to the last decimal, but I hope they are roughly in the right range. The post-2010 numbers have been put together by Singapore-based consulting firm Media Partners Asia.

business story in India. It was the first one my editors asked me to do as soon as I got back.[4]

Star's rise had begun, and it would not stop for six long years. It began with the coming of the irrepressible James Murdoch in Hong Kong, then slowed down and collapsed when he went off to head BSkyB in the UK in 2003. It would rise again when he was back in charge of the Fox business in this part of the world in 2009.

The making of *Kaun Banega Crorepati*

Pratim Mukerjea became 'Peter' when he moved to England with his doctor father, sometime in the 1970s. He'd studied at the prestigious Doon School in India before moving to the UK where he completed his school and college education. He studied business management. Mukerjea then worked with (among others) food major Heinz in the UK and later DDB Needham in Hong Kong where he handled the Star account for Richard Li.

He became CEO of Star in 1999 at age forty-five. (See Chapter 5, 'Star Speaks in Hindi'.) Mukerjea spent much of his first year as CEO cleaning out the stables by having an audit done and ratifying the books. He was worried about skeletons emerging from the closet. Simultaneously, he put together a fantastic team that worked well together—probably his most important contribution to Star's success. 'Peter always hired people better than himself. He would let people fly because he was confident, a team player,' says Sumantra Dutta, who was then part of the ad sales team. Mukerjea had a reputation for being a hard taskmaster but good at delegating authority.

There is, however, another school of thought among old Star hands. That Mukerjea hired as he did because he was essentially an ad salesman and didn't know enough about the other parts of the business. 'To run a business, I believe you need to have a pretty

---

4   'Sixty Minutes That Saved Star' was the headline of the story I did on Star for (then) ABP's *Businessworld*.

strong commercial sense more than content sense. I don't buy programming, unlike my predecessor [Basu] who was very involved with the process. I knew that I did not want to do that because there are experts in the field and you can hire them. I get involved from a broader, strategic perspective. For example, if we take out the news at 9 p.m. what is the financial impact? Positive or negative? And for how long? I don't sit there and say that let us do a drama and let us do it with this producer,' said Mukerjea to me in August 2000 when I asked him about his lack of programming experience.[5]

In any case, this approach stood him and Star in very good stead. The team he put together has given a disproportionate number of CEOs to the Indian media industry. It included a new chief financial officer (R.S. Narayan), a head of business development (Kaushal Dalal) and a new head of distribution (Arun Mohan). Raj Nayak was the ad sales head for all English channels (Star News, Star Movies and Star World). Dutta was made ad sales head for the flagship Star Plus, which would soon become a twenty-four-hour Hindi channel. Sameer Nair was the new programming head. By July 1999, Star was ready to put together its plan for Hindi programming.

Nair, thirty-four, was key to this. An easygoing man who loves a laugh, he had done everything from selling chicken rolls and yellow pages to being an adman before he joined Star TV in 1994 as a producer-director for interstitials for Star Movies. Interstitials are pieces of content that fill the breaks during a film. It could be behind-the-scenes stuff or interviews with the stars. By 1996, under Basu, he was producing shows such as *The Bhaskar Ghose Show*. A year later, he was head of promos and presentation for Star Plus, the flagship channel, and also handled movie acquisition. But till then he had always been on the fringes of the action.

---

[5] Since Peter Mukerjea is currently in jail, interviewing him for this book proved to be difficult. I have quoted him extensively from the interactions I had with him between 2000 and 2006 while covering media for (then) ABP's *Businessworld* magazine.

When Mukerjea was trying to figure out who to hire as head of programming, Shashanka Ghosh and several others recommended Nair. He was a creator and a producer, so he knew both ends of the game. In February 1999, when he was finally made programming head, he kicked off a lot of shows that were 'much appreciated and applauded but got us no ratings,' says Nair. There was *Rajdhani*, a political drama à la *House of Cards*. There were the Star Bestsellers, one-hour films from directors who now rank among India's biggest, including Imtiaz Ali and Rajkumar Hirani. Star Plus did comedy, fiction and talk shows. However, nothing hit the big time.

Around then, Steve Askew, the tall Australian programming head for the region and Nair's boss in Hong Kong, came across *Who Wants to Be a Millionaire*. 'It was very popular [in the UK and Australia] and not at all elitist. It didn't exclude people. People with average intelligence, like me, or the next viewer could watch and enjoy it equally,' said Askew.[6] The game show devised by David Briggs puts regular people selected through various rounds on a hot seat, where they answer fifteen questions. It starts with simple questions and a small amount of prize money, which rises dramatically after each round as the questions get tougher. At several points in the game the person on the hot seat can take his or her winnings and leave.

In July 1999 Askew showed a tape of the show to Nair. 'He saw what I saw,' said Askew. 'I said it was damn good, but it doesn't work for us because of this half-Hindi, half-English limitation,' says Nair. By August, Zee had filed a suit against Star and by October it was clear that a separation was imminent. Star could finally do programming in Hindi. Nair moved fast. He asked Askew to buy the rights for *Who Wants to Be A Millionaire* from ECM, the firm that had bought the Asian rights from format creator Celador. He then started looking around for someone to make a show like that in India.

---

[6]   Steve Askew has been quoted from an interview with me in 2000. He did not respond to my request for an interview for this book.

He zeroed in on Siddhartha Basu. Siddhartha had worked with Star Plus earlier on *A Question of Answers*, a current affairs show with journalist Vir Sanghvi, and on *Eureka*, a science show. A postgraduate in English literature, Siddhartha turned to documentary film-making and then quizzing in the early days of DD. By the time Nair began putting together his team for *Who Wants to Be a Millionaire*, Siddhartha was already a big name on Indian television. He and his wife Anita Kaul-Basu had set up a production firm, Synergy Communications, in 1988. It was producing, among other things, *Mastermind India* on BBC World. Just as the new millennium rolled in, Nair called Siddhartha to check whether Synergy could produce a show like *Who Wants To Be A Millionaire*. 'The prospect of getting our teeth into something so large was interesting. We were up for it,' says Siddhartha.

Askew, Nair and Siddhartha met in January 2000 at the Oberoi hotel in New Delhi to talk about who would host the show. For Nair, 'Amitabh Bachchan was the only choice.' India's biggest superstar at the time was fifty-seven and on the wane. His films had been flopping and he had no connect with a new generation of Indians. Still, his was a name almost every Indian knew and then some. 'When he said "Bachchan" I said perfect— bilingual eloquence, gravitas, mass connect. At that time there were only two icons: [cricketer] Sachin Tendulkar and Amitabh Bachchan. And the formula for non-fiction game shows was cheap and simple. Using Bachchan was to signify scale,' says Siddhartha. 'Scale' was a word that would keep coming back as Star reinvented itself as a fully Hindi, fully local broadcaster. Bachchan was a way of announcing that.

Mukerjea's brief to his marketing team perfectly captured what Star was attempting: 'Think of it as an Indo-Pak one day international [cricket] final; that is the kind of impact I want.' An India–Pakistan cricket match usually brings India to a standstill. The rivalry between the two nations has run deep ever since they were cleaved into separate countries from the same land mass in 1947. It has the kind of nation-stopping impact of a political assassination or that the Super Bowl had in the American market in those days. This was a make-or-break moment for everyone at Star TV.

'We needed to pull together one show that worked across all audience groups, all socio-economic groups and several languages and do it quickly. There wasn't a drama, a soap, a serial or a chat show that could do that. When you look at that kind of brief, you had to find the common denominator across that delivers audiences from kids to grandparents,' said Mukerjea of the task his team faced in 1999.

While they were still talking, late in February 2000, Murdoch senior came to town after four long years. And in a meeting that has now become part of corporate legend, he changed everything. (See Prologue.) He upped the prize money by about a hundred times, made it an hour-long daily show instead of a half-hour weekly show. The name of the show then changed from *Kaun Banega Lakhpati* to *Kaun Banega Crorepati*. For most middle-class Indians, Rs 1 lakh or Rs 1,00,000 was a huge amount; it still is for large swathes of Indians. A prize money of Rs 1 crore or Rs 10 million was something many of us would not save in a lifetime. Murdoch egged the India team on to bet big on getting the largest audience possible, beating the competition by a huge margin and then staying there. By March 2000 the Star team had all the ammo it needed—a great idea for a show, plus Murdoch's backing.

Getting the Big B was proving to be difficult, however. Nair called Sunil Doshi, Bachchan's agent, man about town and now a producer of some repute, and sent him the tapes.[7] 'Amitabh didn't have work, nobody wanted to work with him. The market thought he was finished and the family was against it,' remembers Doshi. 'He was interested but he kept see-sawing,' says Nair. Many meetings followed. Bachchan may have been down and out, but he was the equivalent of Marlon Brando or Al Pacino in India—not the sort of guy who would host a TV show. Not just Bachchan, at that time no Indian film star worth their salt would be seen on television

---

[7]   Sunil Doshi went on to produce *Bheja Fry* and *Bioscopewala*.

unless they had given up on getting film work—it was seen as a step down. Bachchan was understandably ambivalent.[8] Not surprisingly, the Aussie and English expats in Star's Hong Kong office couldn't understand why Bachchan was thinking twice—Hindi cinema was not yet the global force it was to become in the years to come. Nair was adamant on Bachchan, and even Mukerjea, who had no feel for Indian cinema, knew that getting him would make the big difference. He went along with Nair's judgement. But they were already in April. James was keen on closing the deal so that Synergy could start with the rehearsals and Star could launch its flagship show announcing its Hindi avatar soon.

In the process of convincing Bachchan, Nair, Siddhartha, Doshi, Deepak Sehgal, Ravi Menon (part of the programming team) and Dutta took him to London to illustrate what the show was about. Bachchan spent a full day in Elstree Studios on the sets of the UK version of *Who Wants to Be A Millionaire*, which was being hosted by Chris Tarrant. He saw for himself the drama, the scale and the involvement the show created. That evening, Bachchan met with the rest of the team in a suite at the St James's Court hotel in central London, where they were all staying.

Here is how Siddhartha relates what happened next. Bachchan was quiet for some time. Then he turned to Nair and asked, 'Can you do it exactly like the Brits?' Nair turned to Siddhartha. 'My worry was whether the stakeholders would wrap their heads around what was involved. The technology, the telephone issues and the participants—those were my problems. We used to handle very complex shoots on shoestring budgets. So we could do it but "if you give me the resources", I told Sameer. And Star pulled out all the stops.'

Bachchan signed on in April, three months after Nair had first approached him. It was the same month that I had the interview with James and Mukerjea. Another big effort lay ahead to fulfil the promise

---

[8] Amitabh Bachchan did not respond to my request for an interview for this book. I did, however, interview him on the sets of *KBC* in 2000.

of the show and the one made to Bachchan and Siddhartha—putting together the back end for *KBC* in India where production standards were far from world class and infrastructure was wanting. The *KBC* format with its call-ins, SMS voting et al. needed a backbone and IT infrastructure that could take a certain load and could be scaled up. It needed intelligent lighting, continuous electricity—things that were not the norm in India. In April 2000, India had just over 32 million landlines and maybe a couple of million mobile users against over a billion now. A lot of work went into meeting the right people in the government and in telecom companies so that a good back end could be set up. Synergy's team relocated to Mumbai from Delhi and a team of about 250 to 300 people started working on *KBC*. The sets (designed by ace set designer Nitin Desai), the floor lighting, the chair, the computer—all of it—was put together according to the bible that Celador provided and was of a quality that Indian audiences and even the crew had never experienced.

The team was right to worry, worry, worry. When the phone lines opened the per day call volume was over 150 per cent of what the system was designed to handle. An estimated 1.2 million calls were received before shooting for the show began at a specially constructed set at Mumbai's Film City in June 2000. When Bachchan entered the set on the first day of the shoot, all the lights went off. There had been a big technical fault somewhere and all of Mumbai was on the blink. After a wait of three hours the shoot was cancelled. 'Amitabh thought it was a bad omen,' remembers Doshi.

It was probably some of the residual bad luck that Star had had in India. When I asked James how Star could hope to catch up on nine years of being a laggard, he said, 'We did lose a lot of momentum and were hindered terribly because of our partnership with Zee. The restriction on Hindi-language programming was ridiculous. We got out of it at the end of January this year [operationally]. Now we have been going full throttle to build our Hindi programming. I think with the investments and management Peter is putting together, their heads are just going to spin. Sony and Zee won't know what hit them.'

They didn't.

Amitabh Bachchan brings in the billions

On a rainy Monday night on 3 July 2000 at 9 p.m., Indian homes tuned in to Star Plus to Bachchan's baritone announcing, 'Main Amitabh Bachchan bol raha hoon aur aap dekh rahein hain *Kaun Banega Crorepati*.' The biggest shows then, *Amaanat* and *Hasratein* on Zee and *Dastaan* on Sony, did between nine and fifteen on the rating charts.[9] Within the first week *KBC* hit a rating of ten. By August that year it had crossed eighteen. '*KBC*'s impact was like Michael Jackson's *Thriller*—immediate and overpowering. We were one, two, three, four, all within a week,' says Nair, using an analogy he has used countless times to describe the impact that the show had.

There has never been a show like that on Indian television—not until or since then. Some of the biggest hits pre-*KBC*, *Mahabharata* and *Ramayana*, were traffic-stoppers. These had a reach (and therefore viewership since there were no ratings) of 80 per cent in a much smaller, one-channel market in the 1980s. *KBC* did something like that in a competitive market with 100 channels. And it did this on a channel that the masses didn't care about. It united the whole country at 9 p.m. 'Computerji' and 'lock kiya jaaye' became buzzwords in shops, restaurants and regular conversation. 'Even Ganpati pandals starting using *KBC* motifs,' remembers Siddhartha. 'It is not the money but the drama,' Paul Smith, founder of Celador, which owned the format, had said about *Who Wants to Be a Millionaire*. And the drama had us in its thrall. 'The streets would be empty, restaurants empty, it was a wonderful experience,' says Siddhartha.

The money started pouring in. Advertisers were sponsoring everything from the chequebook used to give the prize money to the pen and computer. The average rates for a ten-second spot on

---

[9] A rating point is a weighted average of the time spent by an individual watching a show. So it considers both the number of people and the amount of time spent watching a show.

really popular programmes then varied between Rs 1 lakh and Rs 2 lakh ($2133 to $4266). On *KBC* they went to Rs 3 lakh ($6399) for a ten-second spot. Remember, this was inelastic inventory. Most broadcasters stretch the ad seconds way beyond the standard twelve minutes per hour if a show is working well. The idea is to milk a hit. However, Star, though an underdog, refused to stretch inventory even in its worst year. It was a policy cast in stone. Mukerjea was adamant on not allowing the earnings on every ten seconds of advertising time sold to go down. Besides, expanding inventory would have killed the aura of premiumness Star Plus had ever since it began as an English channel. As a result, advertisers willing to pay Rs 4.5 lakh ($9599) per ten seconds were being turned away. Murdoch called Mukerjea to congratulate him, emphasizing that Star needed to maintain the momentum.

Bachchan, Mukerjea, Nair, the whole team were over the moon when I met them over one intense week of reporting on a cover story on Star in August 2000. Nair was worrying about an array of unexpected problems. The telephone system for *KBC*, meant to take 40,000 calls a day, was getting more than 5 lakh calls. Star tackled that by increasing the capacity and limiting the time for phone-ins. The tough part was the litigation. For a country with a very slow legal system, Indians' love for litigation is amazing. In August 2000 there were half a dozen public interest litigations or PILs filed against *KBC* for really weird reasons. One man in Indore said he wanted Rs 10 crore (over $2 million) in damages for stress because watching the show made him want to participate; and since he couldn't he was stressed! Another said, strangely enough, that *KBC* offended the dignity of women. Then there were prank calls. You could get a call saying that you had been selected for *KBC* and turn up at the studio to discover that it was not so simple. There were quizzes at two levels of selection before you could become a part of the select ten in an episode. And if the show ran out of time before you could participate in an episode, you had to apply all over again.

'*KBC* did for us what we expected it to: it said we were a twenty-four-hour Hindi channel,' said Dutta. This transformation redefined Indian media and broadcasting—its power equations, audience expectation, ideas of scale, everything. 'When *KBC* happened, my people were sleeping. Maybe we made a mistake,' concedes Chandra. More than eight years of success, a string of hit shows and a leading share of audience under its belt had made Zee arrogant, reckon industry people from that time. 'The whole tone of the organization had changed with ad agencies and advertisers. People would wait for hours to see a two-bit associate producer,' says Meenakshi Menon (Madhvani then). She had worked with Zee in its early days. By the time *KBC* happened she had set up and was running Carat India, a media buying agency.

'Before *KBC*, Star was not even considered a competitor. It was Sony versus Zee till 2000. *KBC* was Peter's moment. Star jumped from nowhere to 60-70 per cent of the ad pie overnight,' admits the large, aggressive Kunal Dasgupta who was then CEO of Sony. There were calls and a handwritten note from Murdoch for Mukerjea and some members of his team.

According to Mukerjea, the big gamble was not putting *KBC* on. It was to replace the 9 p.m. news, which brought in over a third of the channel's revenues. 'It was the time our competitors had some of their beefiest shows,' said Mukerjea. Dasgupta remembers that the Sony team assumed *KBC* would be a weekly, as *Millionaire* was the world over. So even if it worked one day, the other evenings *Heena*, *Aahat* and Sony's other popular shows would get in the audiences, and revenues would thus be protected. Murdoch's bet of airing the show four times a week and taking it to sixty minutes created a four-day roadblock in prime time.

'*KBC* scheduled for one show per week wasn't going to work at all. Zee would have simply scheduled a big movie against the show and pulled viewers. We had to schedule *KBC* in such a way that neither Zee nor Sony could ever hope to combat it for any continuing length of time. By scheduling *KBC* for thirteen weeks at the rate of four nights per week, we simply shut out the competition. There weren't fifty-two movies that they could buy and schedule against us night after night,' says a senior manager from that time.

Zee and Sony lost ad share and ratings. They were busy adjusting programming schedules and announcing similar shows. Sony launched *Jeeto Chappad Phad Ke* with film star Govinda as host, while Zee did the hastily thought-through *Sawaal Dus Crore Ka*. Neither worked.

To make matters worse, on the same day as *KBC* came *Kyunki Saas Bhi Kabhi Bahu Thi*, a daily soap at 10.30 p.m. on Star Plus. Sony had a popular show, *Ek Mahal Ho Sapnon Ka*, at 10.00 p.m. those days and Star didn't want to pit anything against it. By October that year it had the confidence to do that and launched another daily show, *Kahaani Ghar Ghar Kii*, at 10 p.m.

Then, as Dasgupta puts it, 'the whole game changed'.

Tulsi Virani joins the party

Ekta Kapoor made her first show for DD in the 1990s, when she was a teenager. *Padosan* was followed by *Mano Ya Na Mano* on Zee TV in 1995. Success came with *Hum Paanch*, a sitcom about a man with five daughters, which became a hit on Zee TV. Balaji Telefilms, the firm she set up with her mother Shobha Kapoor in 1994, was off to a good start. Television was expanding and there was a demand for show ideas and producers. As the daughter of Jeetendra, a top film star of the 1960s, Kapoor belonged to the world of content and loved it. She was making shows for channels across the country. *Koshish: Ek Aasha*, the struggle of the wife of a mentally challenged man, and *Ghar Ek Mandir*, a show she did in Tamil and then in Hindi, were all hugely successful.

'But I wanted to do a daily prime-time soap opera and wasn't getting the chance,' remembers Kapoor, now in her early forties. Dailies were usually telecast in the afternoon and were meant for female audiences. The prime-time audience was the entire family; it still is. Somewhere in February or March of 2000 she met Nair and pitched the idea of a daily prime-time soap, *Kyunki Saas Bhi Kabhi Bahu Thi*. The idea: examine what happens when a daughter-in-law becomes a mother-in-law. When the tapes of the first four episodes landed in the Star office in June, 'I told my programing team, "Don't react to this, we are too intellectual",' laughs Nair. *Kyunki* was bright, garish and over the top going by the standards of the shows airing those days.

'Till 1998–99 Hindi television was still niche, SEC A [socio-economic classification A or upper class] with shows like *Saans, Kora Kagaz*. It was about rich families, divorce. We had commissioned some shows like *Rajdhani*, a political thriller with Bobby Bedi, but not mass TV,' says Tarun Katial, who was then part of the programming team at Star. He went on to become the CEO of Reliance Broadcast Network and later of Zee5, Zee's online video brand.

Till then Hindi shows had a very upper-middle-class feel. The big hits were *Tara*, about a single woman's struggles; *Saans*, about a broken marriage; and *Banegi Apni Baat*, a story of three sisters who are as different as can be, and the paths their lives take. These shows had realistic stories about people who were well educated and sought a solution through hard work and intelligence. This appealed to the audience till the late 1990s. This is because the homes cable TV reached were in buildings in Mumbai, Chennai and Bangalore and in upper-income housing colonies in Delhi, Pune and other cities. However, when *KBC* hit the screens, India was at a massive 33 million cable homes out of a total of 73 million TV families. In other words, just under half the 350 million people watching TV in India had access to cable TV. It was spreading to small towns, semi-urban areas, even metro slums. These shows were very good but did not have quite the mass appeal that, say, Indian films, our most popular form of entertainment, had.

It was this market that Tulsi Virani walked into at 10.30 p.m. on the same night that Bachchan did in July. The daughter-in-law of a typical Gujarati family, she lived with all its members under the same roof. *Kyunki* captured the politics of an Indian family with all its relatives, cousins, uncles and aunts thrown in. The women stood up for issues, they manipulated the men and used their seniority and relationships to get what they wanted. And they did all this while being impeccably dressed, be it in the kitchen or in bed. *Kyunki* was kitchen politics, family machinations and a fashion show all rolled in one. Think of *Dynasty* or *Dallas*, Indianize them with a large joint family, take out all the sex, add lots of colourful clothes and jewellery and you had *Kyunki*.

I started watching it sometime in September 2000 and continued to follow it for five years, maybe more, as did large parts of Hindi-speaking India. *Kyunki* touched something very deep, very basic in us—our insecurities as women in an Indian family and how these play out. In a few months it had overtaken *KBC* in ratings. In October 2000 *Kahaani Ghar Ghar Kii*, another daily soap opera from the Balaji stable, this one about a north Indian joint family, went on-air at 10 p.m. It too became a hit. Star quickly developed a vice-like grip on Indian audiences from 9 p.m. to 11 p.m. Kapoor, now crowned the drama queen of India, continued to create a string of shows that featured strong female protagonists, up to shenanigans of one kind or the other. Invariably these shows started with the letter 'K', since she had become superstitious about the success of *Kyunki* and *Kahaani*. Soon *Kasautii Zindagii Kay*, *Ssshhhh . . . Koi Hai* among many others followed.

'My objective was that after one year of being a 100 per cent Hindi channel, I must be at least at the same level as Zee and Sony in audience share,' Mukerjea had told me then. The reality was even better. By mid-2001, of the top fifty shows in cable homes every week, thirty-nine were on Star Plus. Its share of audience was three times that of Zee, which had plummeted to less than half its pre-*KBC* levels. It had just one show—*Amaanat*—in the top ten now. Sony fell too, but not as severely as market leader Zee. *Heena*, *Aahat* and *CID* among its popular shows continued to hold their own. Soon after *KBC* began airing the Zee stock was hammered, wiping out about 75 per cent of its market capitalization then. The company lost scores of senior managers, and every project and fundraising activity that Chandra had announced was in jeopardy. A lot of this was to do with its own ambition and ability to execute, but Star's success also meant the market saw revenues heading elsewhere. In an interview Chandra gave us at *Businessworld* magazine he said in his brutally honest manner, 'We have gone wrong, we know where we have gone wrong and are taking corrective action.'[10]

'Zee started pushing Zee Cinema, we pushed [Sony] Max, we bought sports. Zee went regional. Till 2004–2005 the Star roadblock continued,' says Dasgupta. By the end of the financial year in June 2001 Star India was at about $241 million (Rs 1130 crore) in revenues. Much of this came from just three shows—*KBC, Kyunki and Kahaani.*

This merited a comment from the senior Murdoch in the 2001 annual report. 'Star increased its operating income by nearly 24 per cent on the strength of advertising gains across its Asian markets—particularly in India, where Star Plus broadcast the vast majority of the country's most popular shows. Led by Star Plus's remarkable advertising gains and threefold increase in viewers, results increased substantially across Star businesses,' said Murdoch in his letter to shareholders. By the end of fiscal 2002 Star Plus was averaging forty of the top fifty shows in cable homes. This also helped it get more money from cable operators—euphemistically called pay revenues in India. Star Asia posted its first-ever operating profit of $2.4 million (about Rs 115 crore) in the January–March 2002 quarter, largely on the back of the India operation. By then the Indian market had expanded to 41 million cable homes out of a total of 82 million TV homes. The variety of programming on satellite channels was tempting more Indians to come on board.

Bachchan's career was resurrected and he continues to do phenomenally well even now, at the age of seventy-six. He still does *KBC*, now on Sony, and some of the choicest film projects go to him. This lift-off from Star helped Kapoor make Balaji Telefilms India's largest TV production firm, which it continues to be. From being the nerdy son, James began to be taken seriously within the News Corp system after the Star success. And when the time came for a

---

[10] Interview with Subhash Chandra in November 2000 for a story in ABP's *Businessworld* issue dated 4 December 2000.

quick change at the crucial BSkyB business, he was made the CEO on the back of what India had achieved. Synergy still does *KBC*, seventeen years after its first show, though it is a Reliance Group firm now. The content and broadcasting ecosystem gained, as did the market, audiences, broadcaster, producers, cable operators—everybody got something.

7

The Making of India's Largest Media House

Social schizophrenia, India's first private FM radio station, a marriage and a divorce

Tulsi Virani, Parvati Agarwal and their ilk provoked a new discussion in India. In the editorial meetings at *Businessworld* where I worked, in magazines and newspapers and at conferences there was scathing contempt for these 'regressive' shows. Some of this was born from News Corp's reputation for dumbing down content, especially when it came to news. The more successful the shows became, the greater the disdain they attracted from certain sections of society.

'How can you bear to watch them?' was a question people like me were asked ad nauseam. My answer, in columns, panel discussions and on TV shows, was always the same. To people who grew up in liberal, open environs, the shows may have seemed 'regressive'. However, they represented a life that was a reality for millions of people. What else could explain the social schizophrenia of a largely left-liberal media dismissing the serials as rubbish and the viewership ratings, which showed that huge parts of India—men and women in urban and rural India—were utterly engrossed in them?

Millions of viewers were cheering Tulsi and Parvati as they battled their in-laws. They rooted for Kkusum when she walked out of her messy marriage. They hoped that Kum Kum would get over her dead husband and find a new mate in life. Even my hyper-conservative mum would get angry when Prerna's husband stopped her from visiting a son, born earlier out of wedlock, in *Kasautii Zindagii Kay*.

Sneering at them was not just intellectual snobbery but a denial of the social context in which Indians lived. There was stigma attached to divorce, widowhood or an illegitimate child in large parts of India. There still is, albeit less so. The fact is that inter-caste and inter-faith marriages are taboo in much of India. Honour killings are carried out not just within India but also by Indians who live abroad. The relationship between a mum-in-law and her daughter-in-law is one of the thorniest to manage in a country like India where the family is part of the package deal in any marriage.

Kyunki, *Kahaani* and the other shows were loud, garish and melodramatic—a bit like Hindi films in the 1980s. But in their own way, within the realm of popular entertainment and the society that they served, they pushed the social envelope bit by bit.

Note that India is overwhelmingly a single-TV-home market. Even when they can easily afford to, Indian homes do not buy a second TV set because they genuinely believe that a family that is entertained together every evening stays together. As a result, even twenty-eight years after satellite television came to the country, only 2 per cent of India's (now) 197 million TV homes have more than one TV. What this means is that all these ideas—a widow in a conservative Rajasthani family getting remarried, a daughter taking financial care of her family, a woman standing up to a domineering husband or to in-laws—were being absorbed by entire families together. The shows planted an idea and brought hope and courage to millions of people who lived with these issues.

I was often booed for defending these TV tales till research bore me out. A study of 2700 households in 180 villages in Bihar, Goa, Haryana, Tamil Nadu and Delhi from 2001 to 2003 by Robert Jensen of Brown University and Emily Oster of the University of Chicago showed that TV soaps were helping rural Indian women to come out of their social shell. Among the things 'The Power of TV: Cable Television and Women's Status in India', released in 2007, showed was that women's preference for male children fell by 12 percentage points after a village got cable TV. There was change too in how women felt about men beating them, something that had been considered acceptable in many of those villages until then.[1]

The fact is, for better or for worse, cable and satellite television was changing India. And Star was a big part of that transformation. Not just that, within the media business, 'KBC changed the way people looked at India, it was a massive moment,' says Vivek Couto. It showcased the potential of the world's second-most populated country as a media market. Because Murdoch and News Corp had done that showcasing, Star and KBC got a huge amount of international media and investor attention. 'The global perception started to turn around 2001 or so. That is when we tried to create SkyGlobal by merging all the satellite TV companies. James and I went to a lot of potential investors in Asia and India as well,' says Bruce Churchill, then deputy CEO, Star Group.

To finance News Corp's expansion into Asia, Latin America and Europe, Sky Global Networks was formed. It combined all the firm's satellite and pay TV brands such as BSkyB, Sky Brazil and Star TV, its distribution technology arm NDS, *TV Guide* magazine and a few others. In July 2000, while *KBC* was taking off, Sky filed with the United States Securities and Exchange Commission for an initial public offering for Sky Global, which would then trade on the

---

[1] Robert Jensen, 'The Power of TV: Cable Television and Women's Status in India', School of Public Affairs, UCLA, Watson Institute for International Studies, Brown University and NBER; Emily Oster, University of Chicago and NBER.

New York Stock Exchange. The plan was shelved when News Corp began its attempts to acquire another US-based DTH operator, DirecTV. All the same, the Sky Global prospectus is revealing.

It talks glowingly of India's contribution to Star's total revenues, the growth in the subscription and advertising market, the success of Star News and its imminent break-even. Of all the firms in the Sky Global Network, Star TV was the only asset that News Corp owned 100 per cent. It was, therefore, critical, and one the company was constantly highlighting to analysts and media.

Star had got its lift-off. Now it needed to build a fully fledged media company on the back of it.

'We want to become the No. 1 media company in India,' said Mukerjea in the aftermath of *KBC*.

The first private FM radio station

For a media company in Star's position there were several avenues for growth—get into more genres, markets, businesses or media. Sports, entertainment and news are the three biggest genres that drive growth. This is true not just in broadcasting but also for any media anywhere in the world. In India, the genre opportunity is especially large given the array of languages in which each can be taken. For example, a company could do soaps in Hindi, Tamil, Telugu and Marathi, among a dozen other languages. The same was true for sports and news and even music. These programmes in different languages could be monetized through either advertising or subscription (pay) revenues. They could also become revenue earners in other geographies—as rival Zee would demonstrate through its international bouquet, a huge hit with the Indian diaspora in the UK, the US and elsewhere. There were thus three pivots for growth—more genres, more media and more geography. Star went after most of these.

The first was the Internet.

When Murdoch was in India in late February/early March 2000, he did several things. First, he changed the whole *Kaun*

Banega Lakhpati plan to *Kaun Banega Crorepati* (see Prologue). Second, he visited Bangalore to check out for himself the thing that was exciting investors and analysts around the world—the Internet. Their enthusiasm had created pressure on News Corp's print- and TV-heavy portfolio. There was a sense that it was not doing enough to invest in 'new media'. In Bangalore, Murdoch met with Pradeep Kar of Microland, a mover and shaker in the dotcom world. Microland had set up several websites and was planning more. Sunil Lulla, now group CEO of Balaji Telefilms and an old media hand, was then with Microland. He made the first presentation on Indya. com to Murdoch and his team of a dozen people including lawyers. Indya.com was planned as a horizontal portal that would provide news, travel, tickets, everything. Think of Rediff plus Amazon in the current era. 'He [Murdoch] said I like what I see, we shook hands and the deal was signed,' says Lulla.

In that year, News Corp picked up stakes in several Internet start-ups in India, spending over $100 million (Rs 469 crore) over ten weeks. There was ITSpace, a business-to-business portal on information technology (another Microland launch), Egurucool, Indiaproperties, Explocity and Bazee, an e-commerce site, among others. The biggest was the $50 million (Rs 234 crore) spent on a 37.5 per cent stake in Indya.com. It was launched in April 2000 with James in attendance. 'We think the Indian media business and digital economy is at an inflection point,' he said.

By 2001, dotcom valuations crashed. So did scores of fledgling firms, many with flimsy business plans. The bubble had burst. A shareholders' rearrangement at Microland meant News Corp had to take over Indya.com completely. None of the investments made in Internet companies in early 2000 had delivered. Both Internet speed and penetration in India were pathetic. There were less than half a million people with Internet access and most of this was of the narrowband, dial-up type. The idea of buying things online just didn't make sense because even in the metros Internet speeds were so poor that consumers had to wait a long time for a simple page of content to download. Still, the excitement of a new medium, the

AOL–Time Warner merger and the promise of a new dawn had investors madly excited—especially because TV was doing so well in India. 'Many years later James said, "Sunil, we were not wrong, just ahead of our time",' recalls Lulla.

The Indya.com episode, however, is an important first stop in Star's journey to create Hotstar, now among India's largest streaming apps. Indya.com continued to mark Star's online presence for years.

The second opportunity Star went after, with better success, was radio.

James was particularly excited about it, says Sumantra Dutta. In 1993 the Indian government had allowed private FM operators to take blocks on the state-owned AIR. The Times Group launched Times FM, and Tariq Ansari's tabloid *Mid-Day* did Radio Mid-Day.[2] The business grew rapidly, pushing ad revenues for radio from Rs 58 crore ($18 million) in 1993 to Rs 93 crore ($24 million) in 1997–98. Somewhere in the middle of 1998, the Prasar Bharati chief, M.S. Gill, decided to push private operators out. However, lobbying by a clutch of twenty-four media companies that formed the Radio Group helped. The government decided to privatize FM radio. A messy, open auction in March 2000 resulted in 108 licences being issued. Of these, six went to Music Broadcast Private Limited, a firm owned by steel magnate Laxmi Mittal's brother Pramod Mittal. Star became the managing agency—handling technology, marketing and programming. It was a back-door entry into radio because foreign firms were not allowed to invest under the radio policy.

John Catlett, an international radio professional, was brought in as CEO and Dutta moved in as COO of Star India's radio division. Dutta was superstitious about 3 July, the date *KBC* had launched. So on 3 July 2001, Radio City, India's first private FM radio station, started broadcasting from Bangalore. The CEO of almost every company that owned a licence was parked in Bangalore that week,

---

[2]   *Mid-Day* is now owned by Jagran Prakashan Limited, a large publishing firm that dominates the Hindi-speaking market.

listening in. The speed with which Radio City got off the ground came from News Corp's international heft, which it had brought to India once again. The station brought in audio serials and also audio versions of Star's popular shows—*Saans, Kora Kagaz* and *KBC*. Within three years. Radio City was at Rs 72 crore ($16 million) in revenues—that is, three-fourths of the market size at the time the auctions began. But its backdoor entry into radio and subsequent success made the government, justifiably, upset. And it jeopardized Star's second attempt at DTH, as we will see.

The third opportunity was distribution—both DTH and cable. In September 2000, Star paid Rs 251 crore ($75 million) for 26 per cent of Hathway Cable, India's second-largest cable network, reaching 2.5 million homes. 'When we came away from the Siticable and Zee relationship the market assumed that we were walking away from distribution and would therefore have a tough time. We have to have a certain amount of leverage in distribution and access and better placement on the channel spectrum,' Mukerjea had explained to me around that time. Hathway, said analysts, was a hedge against a potential blackout by Siticable or others. What continued to interest News Corp, though, was DTH.

The quest for pay revenues

For Star, cable or DTH has never been so much about controlling distribution as it has been about pay revenues. It was about bringing the India operation on a par with the other, largely developed, markets it operated in. Globally, most developed markets then got 70 per cent or more of their revenues from pay—which explains why it is known as the pay-TV business. That is what keeps broadcasting healthy and pushes up programming quality. In India, the cable route, which controlled 33 million of India's 73 million TV homes in 2000 was—and still is—an opaque mess. Of the Rs 3960 crore ($897 million) collected on the ground then, very little, maybe 10 per cent, would have gone back to broadcasters.

There were three reasons for this. One, most channels were unencrypted, free-to-air and dependent on ad revenues. Two, local cable operators routinely under-declared the number of subscribers they had. Three, the business of collecting subscription fees from homes was—and still is—primarily cash-based. Much of this leaks out of the system. Star had made serious inroads into the pay market, getting an estimated Rs 110 crore ($23.4 million) in the financial year ended 2000. That was about 10 per cent of its estimated top line that year. The hope was to push the figure to roughly half of all revenues, eventually overtaking ad revenues. The idea behind investing in Hathway was also to facilitate the development of distribution into a healthy pay stream.

This, however, was a News Corp ambition. James, Davey, Churchill and many of the expats understood that. They came from markets where there was complete transparency on the ground. Cable was controlled by companies that were on a system (digital or analogue) that declared all consumers, paid taxes on the collected money and gave broadcasters their share.

The money made from pay or cable is referred to as 'affiliate fee' in most global broadcaster balance sheets. In India, because of the mess, the fights and the chaos, the unsavoury nature of cable meant that the 'broadcast business had an implicit caste system where ad sales was seen as superior and distribution as inferior,' explains Paritosh Joshi, who joined Star as president, advertising sales and distribution, in August 2005. Most broadcast CEOs, including Mukerjea, just didn't want to deal with distribution more than was necessary. 'Distribution was always a by-product. Senior management didn't understand how critical distribution was,' affirms Tony D'Silva, who joined in May 2002 as head of distribution for Star.

That also explains in part why sports, which was bringing in good pay revenues, received little attention from Mukerjea and from Star. In October 1996, just when Basu was joining as CEO in India, Star TV Asia had entered into a 50:50 joint venture with Disney's ESPN. Star Sports and ESPN would remain separate channels while the joint venture would control ESPN India, Star Sports

India and the duo's channels in China and Taiwan. ESPN India was an encrypted channel, which sold for Rs 5 (about 15 cents) per subscriber per month. Since the parent firms were fierce rivals in the US and other parts of the world, getting them to work together was difficult for the top management. 'They were two sides with different philosophies and no trust. Still, Bruce [Churchill, deputy CEO, Star Group] was there and ESPN trusted him,' says Rik Dovey, then managing director, ESPN-Star Sports. A big problem was that Star was not interested in distributing the joint venture channels, says R.C. Venkateish, who ran ESPN-Star Sports in India from 2003 to 2010. This, when more than three-fourths of the joint venture firm's $65 million income (half of which went to Star) came from pay revenues in March 2003.

The combination of these factors—the opaque, chaotic mess in cable, Mukerjea's disdain for it, the troubled joint venture with ESPN—ensured that Star did not hit the big numbers on pay revenues for a long time. Nor did it make it big in sports broadcasting, a genre that drives its business in the US and the UK. Star stuck largely to Hindi general entertainment. There was very little sports, language and platform expansion. This proved damaging in the long run.

This lack of focus on pay revenues showed in 2002 when the government made a change to the Cable Television Networks (Regulation) Act, 1995. The CAS or conditional access system amendment made it mandatory to receive pay channels through a set-top box. The intention was good, but it was flawed legislation that was silent on who would bear the cost of the technology and gave the government too much power to decide what channels would be watched, where and at what price. It caused tremendous confusion on the ground. There were blackouts, fights and loads of court cases. And somehow most broadcasters did not come out looking good. They opposed CAS for all the right reasons, but their heart was really not in ensuring full digitization. Most couldn't see beyond the loss of immediate viewership—and therefore ad revenues—as the market transitioned from being free-to-air to going encrypted.

Star, incidentally, was one of those broadcasters. If CAS had been well thought-through and had not been insidiously opposed by broadcasters, the cable market in India could have become a significant revenue generator by now. While DTH is now a huge contributor to pay revenues, cable continues to present difficulties for broadcasters. (See Chapter 11, 'The Star That Shankar Made'.)

Since it was getting one programming hit after another on Star Plus, none of this probably mattered to Mukerjea. It was only when the other genre where Star had made significant inroads, news, was coming apart that time and attention shifted to pay or other revenue streams.

The divorce with NDTV

Murdoch is a news buff. The political and social context of a country and how its news industry operates is one of his favourite topics of conversation. Whenever he travels to any News Corp office around the world, he seeks out editors working for the group and asks them questions around news, society and politics. Uday Shankar, chairman, Star and Disney India, and president APAC, direct-to-consumer and international, The Walt Disney Company, was the CEO for Star News from 2004 to 2007. On one of Murdoch's trips to India in 2005, Shankar took him around the newsroom. 'He asked me questions out of curiosity. In one hour he would have asked hundreds of questions. My memory of him was, "What an incredibly inquisitive man!",' laughs Shankar. In most markets where News Corp had a news presence—Australia, the US, the UK—the rules were clear. In India, they were not. In print, foreign firms had been grudgingly allowed 26 per cent foreign investment in 2002, but the ground rules for news broadcasting were not specified. It was against this backdrop that the differences between Star and NDTV began.

'Although he [Murdoch] financed the channel [Star News] he had no hesitation in giving us total editorial control,' says Prannoy Roy in an essay he wrote in a book commemorating twenty-five years of NDTV.[3] 'The relationship between Star and NDTV was very hands-off. NDTV always had the upper hand. I have no idea what the formal agreement between both the parties was but they used NDTV mikes in reportage [while the channel was Star News] and didn't change even after we protested. You could say they built their brand on the back of Star,' says Dilshad Master-Kumar, senior vice president, operations and programming, Star News. The NDTV-programmed Star News's coverage of the Gujarat riots in 2002 is, in fact, counted amongst the most fearless in the business. It also raised hackles in several quarters including the ruling Bharatiya Janata Party at that time. It brought private news broadcasters firmly on the government's radar. Roy has written in the NDTV book about getting calls to tone down the reportage. This editorial freedom given to an outside programmer was the cause of constant skirmishes between the editorial team at NDTV and the ad sales team at Star India.

Roy and his team brooked no suggestion or attempt to try and change a story or a report they were doing. This rankled for several reasons, the biggest being that Star had paid NDTV an advance (to buy the equipment) plus a fixed fee with a built-in 15 per cent escalation clause. The amount spent in the first year was reportedly $10 million (just over Rs 39 crore). By March 2002 the fee NDTV got amounted to Rs 70 crore (about $14.6 million). Though Star News made an estimated Rs 50 crore ($10 million) in revenues by then, it wasn't profitable. NDTV had no skin in the revenue game. It probably didn't care. But rising year-on-year targets meant the Star team was straining at the leash, wanting some say in shows or content.

With about a year of the five-year contract (1998–2003) left to run, Mukerjea was wondering what to do about this. Star could go with NDTV as it was, or it could find a new firm to replace NDTV, or it could run a news channel itself. It explored various options

---

[3]   Ayesha Kagal, ed., *More News is Good News: Untold Stories from 25 Years of Television News* (Noida: HarperCollins, 2016).

of entering into a joint venture with NDTV. But they couldn't agree on the right to appoint the editor-in-chief of the channel. Roy refused to give up any editorial control. It was while this discussion was going on that something happened to help Mukerjea make up his mind.

In a meeting with a major textile company, which was also an advertiser, Mukerjea faced a piquant question. The chairman and managing director of the Indian textile group had a bone to pick on a news report that had run on Star News. It was about environmental issues in a town where they operated. They insisted that the report was one-sided; the reporter had not taken the firm's views into account. How could a channel that claimed to be unbiased allow this? Mukerjea explained that he had no control over editorial matters. The chief of the textile firm asked him a basic question: who was paying whom? When Mukerjea explained that NDTV was paid an annual fee by Star, he just looked at Mukerjea and said paternally, 'Malik ka koi malik nahi hota [nobody owns the owner].' For him, the channel was owned by Murdoch and Star was responsible.

This was probably the last straw. It hit Mukerjea that whether or not Star had editorial control, to everyone outside it was culpable if something went wrong. He conveyed his apprehensions to James. There had already been a fracas over the *Nikki Tonight* episode in 1995. (See Chapter 5, 'Star Speaks in Hindi'.) 'Editorial independence' then became the deal-breaker in the second round of negotiations. 'Earlier, they [Star TV] had agreed to let NDTV continue to have editorial control. It was on that basis that we agreed to start discussions on continuing/renewing the contract. However, in December 2001, Star TV suddenly changed its mind and said it wanted editorial control. It was then that we decided to break with Star because we believed that NDTV as an Indian company should retain full editorial control,' Roy told me in an email interview later in 2003.

Star decided to do its own news channel. And NDTV started planning two news channels—one in Hindi (NDTV India) and the other in English (NDTV 24X7). Their break-up was amicable according to both firms. However, it had repercussions that went far beyond the launch of a few new channels.

That foreign feeling

In 2002, the Indian news broadcast market was at an interesting stage. What Star News did for English news in 1998, the India Today Group's Aaj Tak had done for Hindi news in 2001. It was the most watched news channel and was earning about Rs 52 crore ($10.8 million) in ad revenues by then. Besides Star News, there were Zee News (Hindi) and Sun News (Tamil), among others. But the real competition would be between the about-to-be launched Star News Hindi, which would be programmed by Star, and Aaj Tak, which was the leader. When Star and NDTV decided to break off, more than a dozen channels, with a total investment of over Rs 500 crore ($100 million plus), were planning to launch in a market that gave Rs 200 crore ($42 million) to news channels in advertising.

From Star's point of view, going on its own signified freedom and lower costs. After the initial investment of about Rs 250 crore ($51 million), it had to spend Rs 35 crore ($7 million) or so every year on programming. Star News would break even in three years. More importantly, it would give Star the freedom to experiment with programming and formats. Mukerjea was keen to get away from mainstream news because that to him was a lightning rod that could attract regulators. The idea was to do a lighter, more tabloid-style news channel out of Mumbai instead of Delhi, the headquarters of the news industry in India. Mumbai was also home to the Hindi film industry, so entertainment and news could be combined. The new Star News would be gunning for a younger audience looking for 'entertaining news'. It was to steer clear of political and current affairs, an area where NDTV was most comfortable. 'The instruction from the boss [Murdoch] was very clear. It would be better for us to be No. 2. It was fine to be No. 1 in entertainment but not in both entertainment and news. We would attract too much attention and that wasn't a good thing for a foreign media company,' says a senior manager from that time.

It proved to be a valid concern. Star's 'foreign' origin reared its head once more. The launch of Star News 2.0 became a nightmare because over a decade after private broadcasting had begun in India, the regulations to deal with such a situation did not exist.

For many years the Indian government did not allow foreign broadcasters to uplink from India. Most sent tapes to Hong Kong or Singapore where the content was packaged with ads and broadcast back into the country. Live news, a market that began with the birth of Star News in February 1998, works best with domestic uplinking—that is, sending programmes up to a satellite, which then beams them down into the target market.

In June 1998, the government allowed Indian companies with Indian equity of not less than 80 per cent and effective management control in Indian hands to uplink from India through Videsh Sanchar Nigam Limited or VSNL (now Tata Communications). This was subject to clearance from the Ministry of Information and Broadcasting. In 1999, the cabinet allowed all Indian broadcast companies to uplink without the mandatory use of VSNL. This was further liberalized in 2000. All broadcasters, irrespective of their ownership and management, were allowed to uplink from India. They had to adhere to all the other norms, such as the advertising and broadcasting code. But by that time most broadcasters had invested in infrastructure abroad and saw no reason to uplink from India.

Star India's application in October 2002 requesting permission to uplink from India for its news channels set the government thinking again. Here was a 100 per cent subsidiary of a $15 billion American media firm wanting to broadcast news in India. As long as NDTV programmed this news, Indian regulators were not overly concerned as NDTV was a 100 per cent Indian firm. The government was uncomfortable with allowing a foreign broadcaster into news. The ministry then decided to make it mandatory for all news broadcasters out of India to uplink from here and limit them to a 26 per cent foreign investment holding cap. The news channels using VSNL to log on to their uplink sites abroad, such as Star or CNBC, were given three months to restructure. Others such as Zee, which uplinked from outside India, had a year to bring down their foreign equity.

The problem was not just the new rule; it was that it was introduced on 26 March, while the channel was to be launched on 1 April. Till the guidelines were issued, Star had no idea if it could even launch because its uplink licence had not been granted. If it could, everything was in place and its first show, *Star Savera*, was set to roll. If not, 300 people who had been employed would lose their jobs. Once it was clear it could launch the channel, Star set about restructuring its news operation. With the help of a variety of people, Star cobbled together a 74 per cent shareholding with Indians. The shareholders were DSP Merrill Lynch chief Hemendra Kothari (25 per cent), *Hindustan Times* editor Vir Sanghvi (5 per cent), film actor and Balaji Telefilms head Jeetendra Kapoor (5 per cent), theatre and television personality Maya Alagh (5 per cent), Star Group legal adviser Raian Karanjawala (4 per cent) and adman Suhel Seth (30 per cent). Star retained the 26 per cent. Since it was an on-air channel, it got permission to continue till it restructured and after that got a transitory uplink licence.

This arrangement, however, was clearly not what the regulators intended. It followed the law technically but flouted it in spirit because Star controlled the news operation. This was all the ammo that competitors needed to fan the 'foreign fire' once more. There was, as discussed in the chapter 'Star Speaks in Hindi', enormous apprehension within government and media circles about Murdoch and News Corp. His print business bothered most Indian media barons. When Star finally got the permission to launch a news channel, several Indian media companies got together to form the Indian Media Group. This included NDTV, Sahara, The Times Group, Living Media and Zee. They lobbied the government to change broadcasting ownership laws. The government agreed.

The uplink guidelines were revised once more on 28 August 2003 to state that at least 51 per cent of a news channel must be owned exclusively by one single Indian entity. Star had to once again dilute the equity of the shareholders, who held 74 per cent. Then it had to find a partner who would take a majority 51 per cent and another who would take the remaining 23 per cent. And it had to do so within a month. Star had until 28 September to meet the new guidelines.

Mukerjea and his team went into hyperactive mode. They had to ensure that Star News did not go off-air. A list of potential partners was put in place. According to media reports from that time, Shobhana Bhartia's Hindustan Times Group and Aveek Sarkar's ABP Group were shortlisted. James then told Mukerjea to state his preference since he would be dealing with this partner. Murdoch met with the owners of both firms in London and finally everyone settled on ABP.

The Kolkata-based media firm had (it still does) the largest-selling Bengali and English newspapers—*Anandabazar Patrika* and the *Telegraph*—in the eastern part of the country. It had several magazines in Bengali and English. It had one national brand, *Businessworld* magazine (which it later sold to Anurag Batra), which I was working for at the time. It was one of the more cerebral and intellectually liberal media firms in the country. And its owner brothers, Aveek and Arup Sarkar, were seen as good old-fashioned print media barons. Aveek (who did not respond to my request for an interview) was and still is an erudite, with-it publisher/editor. Some of India's finest editors—T.N. Ninan, Vir Sanghvi, Tony Joseph, among others—have worked for ABP. It was, I suppose, a good match. Murdoch liked the news business, Aveek was an old-style editor and an anglophile. They each knew their craft and their strengths.

ABP picked up a 74 per cent stake in Media Content and Communication Services or MCCS, the firm that owned Star News. And it gained hugely from it. News broadcasting is now one of its largest and possibly most profitable businesses. I later asked

Mukerjea if NDTV's independent and provocative coverage was the cause of the delay in the uplink and the trouble Star went through in getting permissions. 'I don't know whether it was specifically connected to the uplink permission but it certainly has a role to play in the negative feeling towards Star as a brand. That perhaps reflects in the areas where we need approvals, whether it has to do with DTH or news,' said Mukerjea.

News, however, is what led to the unravelling of Star. Because it was while setting up the news operation that Mukerjea made moves that would haunt the company.

8

Star-crossed

James leaves a rising Star, kitchen politics claims it

James Murdoch surprised me. In an hour-long session with six hard-boiled Indian journalists he didn't once lose his cool. He answered every question with uncanny assurance. From the ratings of *Kasautii Zindagi Kay* to the intricacies of the CAS amendment he knew it all; we scribes had to be careful before asking a question. He even chatted knowledgeably about Mumbai's mass transit problems, amongst a host of other things.

This was May 2002. Star had flown a bunch of Indian journalists to its regional headquarters in Hong Kong. This was when I met James for a second—and once again, extended—time. We met at a small press briefing and then later over lunch where he teased me about my Atkins diet, just as I was reaching for the rice. He'd retained his humour, but gone was the eager schoolboy who'd let slip that News Corp would be investing $125 million in Indian

Internet start-ups during that first interview in April 2000. (See Chapter 6, 'The Sixty Minutes That Saved Star'.) This man parried every question with aplomb and was completely in command of the briefing and the lunch, where all of us bombarded him with questions.

James had grown in years but more importantly in knowledge, understanding and his grasp of the business. There was something else that seemed different about him. First I thought he had grown arrogant with success. Then it hit me that he was just being more careful than before. In the minefield of Asia, something said in India could upset the Chinese and something uttered in Hong Kong could infuriate the Indians. He was twenty-seven when he took over Star Group to the accompaniment of much sniggering within News Corp where elder brother Lachlan was seen as the chosen one. At twenty-nine, international media and analysts were finally looking at him, and therefore India, more seriously.

James's biggest success then was India—the only performing country of any significance in News Corp's Asia portfolio. By its financial year ending June 2003, Star India was at an estimated Rs 1200 crore ($249 million) in revenues, over two-and-a-half times its top line in June 1999 when it started with the Hindi plan. More importantly, it was—along with Zee—a contender to become India's second-largest media company after The Times Group, which was estimated at Rs 1500 crore ($311 million) in the financial year ending March 2003. Zee, at Rs 1286 crore ($267 million), was slightly better than Star on revenues thanks to its success in selling Zee to cable operators in the US, the UK and other countries. However, it had less than a third of Star's viewership in India. Similarly, DD, with a higher reach but just 40 per cent of Star's revenues, didn't make the cut. Star was, decisively, India's second-largest media house—in terms of both audience and revenues. By September 2003, all of the top fifty Hindi programmes in India were those running on Star Plus. It led the ratings and viewership charts by a long shot. It had become what Murdoch wanted, a dominant player invested in India. There was talk of raising money through an initial public offering on the Indian bourses and offering equity options to employees.

Star's rise, however, was not about the rankings. It was first and foremost a vindication of Murdoch's vision; second, it was an awesome display of the Indian market's potential; and third, it was a manifestation of the fundamental shifts in Indian media consumption.

'Within News Corporation, Star was regarded as Rupert's personal fiefdom; and after him, it was James. Both father and son took a direct, personal interest in all things Star to the extent that our relationship with New York/Los Angeles was quite unlike the typical regional executive reporting to the US headquarters like in Disney, Viacom or Sony,' says Sameer Nair. Bruce Churchill reckons it is because 'News Corp is not originally an American company and that is a big difference. A lot of American companies look at the international markets as a sales opportunity. News Corp started in Australia, then built a successful business in the UK and then went to the US. So we knew we could build an international business by going and building local stuff, we didn't take the Australian papers to the UK.' After spending $870 million to buy a firm broadcasting to thirty-eight countries in 1993, being ridiculed for it, and then pouring in an equal amount of money to make those businesses local, Murdoch's Asian adventure finally looked as if it was paying off.

I have read about half a dozen books on Murdoch plus scores of articles and have spoken to dozens of managers within News Corp who have worked with him. The picture that emerges is of a man who has an instinct for the media business, a nose for a good deal and a long-term perspective that most competitors who were wedded to margins lacked. 'In 1997–98 when the Asian financial crisis hit, Rupert lost money. But India stayed the course. They had never seen that kind of success [like *KBC*]. So they doubled down on India and China. They made a strategic investment in Taiwan which was all right and in Indonesia in 2005 but that didn't work out,' says Vivek Couto. Murdoch's letter to shareholders in the 2003 annual report reflects this. 'After years of diligent work, Star celebrated its first full year of operating profitability. By driving up both subscription and advertising revenues while improving efficiency, Star posted a substantial rise in operating income year-over-year,' he wrote. Star India has featured in almost every annual report of News Corp from 2000 onwards.

That brings us to the second reason why the Star success was significant. Its success was written about and underlined in the Mecca of the media business—the US. It meant the redrawing of the global media map to make India (and perhaps Asia) more interesting to investors. India had one of the biggest consumer bases in the world; it had the largest film-producing industry and the third-largest cable market (then). It was also a democracy where free speech, essential for the growth of the media business, was protected. Yet it was not considered a serious player in the international market for media and entertainment. The $249 million in revenue that Star India had delivered was the best possible proof of the country's potential. 'If you can play the game the Indian way, you can win', Star's victory seemed to say. During investor calls, analysts were asking News Corp's senior management about Star India and about the progress of DTH.

Till then, except for Star and Sony, there had been no major foreign investors in Indian media. Viacom had a presence through MTV, Turner through Cartoon Network and CNN. Disney was struggling in a joint venture with Modi Enterprises. With its bureaucracy and anti-foreign sentiments, India was seen as a graveyard for media firms. 'Star has a material impact on how the rest of the world looks at Asian television,' said Janine Stein, editorial director of Singapore-based Television Asia at the time. She later became editor and publisher of ContentAsia. News Corp had successfully showcased the potential of this tough market. Soon, almost every global broadcaster was upping the ante on its Indian investments. For instance, in 2002, Turner entered into a distribution joint venture with Zee. Sony started buying up cricket rights, pushing up prices in the process. It was looking to use sports to tackle Star's hegemony over prime time.

Star's rise also shifted the excitement and buzz of growth away from print media, which had dominated thus far. That TV could be a more powerful medium, especially in a country with low literacy levels (65 per cent in 2001), seems self-evident now. However, in the days of DD and before private channels came on the scene, that was still a theory that needed testing. The rise in the number of TV homes and in the number of people watching cable and satellite TV had a cascading effect on the reach, power, influence and spends of every other media. The overall market expanded. Almost 60 million people watched *Kyunki Saas Bhi Kabhi Bahu Thi* or *Kahaani Ghar Ghar Kii* against the 16.5 million who read *Dainik Jagran*, the largest-selling Hindi newspaper at the time. Indian homes paid an average of Rs 150 ($3.2) as their cable bill every month compared to between Rs 30 and Rs 50 (65 cents to just over $1) for a newspaper.

Like many of my journalist friends then, you could argue that newspaper readership and TV viewership are not strictly comparable. My contention then as now is that every media fights for time and share of wallet from the same consumers and advertisers. In a huge, under-penetrated market like India, the base keeps getting larger. So, while in absolute numbers print continues to grow even today, in percentage terms its share began to decline. When Richard Li sold his business to Murdoch, print's share in India's total ad pie was 60 per cent. By 2003 this was down to 43 per cent. The Times Group had (by then) taken 160 years to reach the scale that Star was very close to achieving in just over a decade. And there was still so much headroom. In 2003, only 80 million of India's 202 million homes had TV. Of these, only 49 million had cable. At an average of five people per household, Star was reaching over 200 million people—and there were about 800 million more to go.

If you read the chapter 'Once Upon a Time . . .' you will remember that Li had offered a transponder to every major print baron in India. But they found it difficult to look beyond the hegemony of their regions and languages or their rankings within English or Hindi or Tamil or Telugu. Very few of them attempted broadcasting. The Hindustan Times, Ushodaya Enterprises (the publishers of *Eenadu*, and Living Media (the publishers of *India Today*) were the honourable exceptions. Star was not just a catalyst for the changes that Indian media was seeing but was also beginning to benefit from them.

Such was the sensitivity to the foreign tag by now that neither Mukerjea nor James wanted to acknowledge Star's rise up the ranks from a has-been to the second-largest media firm in India. I did another cover story on Star in the summer of 2003. When I asked Mukerjea how it felt to be so close to being No. 1, he froze me out. 'When we said that we want to be India's No. 1 media company we were not necessarily saying that it has to be in revenues. We want to be the largest in terms of being in the maximum number of homes in India,' he said. James was friendly but refused to talk for the story. And on a visit to India, the senior Murdoch reportedly slammed a copy of *Businessworld* magazine on a table in the Star office in Mumbai when he saw the headline for my cover story, 'The Making of India's Largest Media House'.

Did the foreign tag bother Mukerjea and Star? 'We are seen and welcomed into most Indian homes that have a cable and satellite connection. If they had any reservations about us being foreign then they wouldn't be watching our soap operas,' said Mukerjea. Then after a pause he added, 'But we are in the media business. That by itself is a sensitive category. If we were laggards, people would not feel threatened. But the fact that we are a leader by some clear distance creates barriers. There is always the Rupert Murdoch tag attached to it. For example, if one of the five members of the Viva band [created though a talent show on Channel [V]] were to leave the band, the headline to the story is "the Rupert Murdoch–controlled . . . pop band loses one of its members". Unfortunately, the Murdoch tag keeps coming in and it has its own feelings of sensitivity. A lot of this is created by the media, which for some reason is worried that Star is part of the News Corporation. And that unless they were to put a stop to it or create an environment where our growth is curtailed either through bad PR or negativism something will happen,' said Mukerjea.

For the CEO of a media company on an all-time high, he was remarkably morose in that interview. But Mukerjea had a point. Kunal Dasgupta too headed a largely foreign media company, Sony, but he did not face the accusation of being 'foreign' in the way that Mukerjea did. Ditto for Turner and Viacom and Disney. They weren't in the news business and they did not have a strong, colourful owner. Star localized and Indianized faster than any other firm—its management, thinking and programming are all local. 'Except for ownership nothing is foreign about Star,' says Punit Goenka, managing director and CEO, Zee Entertainment Enterprises, and Subhash Chandra's son. Sure, Mukerjea is a British citizen, but he is essentially Indian.

You could dismiss the xenophobia as part of an evolving market that was not yet used to foreigners and did not have a robust regulatory framework (it still doesn't) for the media business. There was more to Mukerjea's pessimism than just the travails of a foreign company trying to navigate India's bureaucracy. His winning team was coming apart even as James, his mentor, comrade-in-arms and the man responsible for pushing everything Star India wanted through the News Corp system, was on his way out. In February 2003 James was appointed as a director on the board of the troubled BSkyB. By November he was named CEO of the (then) £3.2 billion pay-TV operator and Britain's nineteenth-largest public limited company, amidst strong opposition from various shareholder groups. The feeling was that Murdoch was pushing his choice of CEO though he had just a 34.5 per cent stake in the firm. James left Hong Kong for London with what was clearly a promotion. He'd done a good job in Asia and had been rewarded.

As you will read later in this chapter, there were many things that led to the near-collapse at Star in 2006. James's going was the biggest blow, say people from that time. 'The first three years were brilliant. James was there, so there was no politics. By the end of 2003 he went to London. Michelle [Guthrie] came. If James had not gone there would neither be the politics nor [the] slowdown,' says Nair.

'There was a collapse of momentum. The energy in the organization vanished and the work culture significantly changed. At Star, James was the creator of the hard-work culture. His proximity to Rupert meant that he was able to get things moving in ways that would be difficult for a mere executive. His departure took with it all plans to take Star public. This slammed the brakes on the enthusiasm among the staff in India [who were looking forward to e-sops],' says one senior manager.

Cracks begin to appear

In late 2001 and early 2002, Mukerjea was scouting around for a head for Star News, the channel it would launch after its break-up with NDTV. Raj Nayak, who was head of ad sales, evinced interest in the job. Mukerjea wanted someone from outside the company. The reasons he gave for this were different to different people— he needed a fall guy if the project failed, he wanted another senior programming person as backup. Whatever the logic, his decision to hire Ravina Raj Kohli didn't go down well with many in the core team.

Kohli (no relation of mine) was the successful former programming head for Sony. She then became CEO of Nine Gold, which won a three-hour slot on DD Metro, DD's then second general entertainment channel (it later became DD News). The slot was licensed to HFCL-Channel Nine Broadcasting, a joint venture between Himachal Futuristic Communications Limited and Australian media baron Kerry Packer's Channel Nine. The slot did very well, but the contract, which ended in October 2001, was not renewed. Kohli had set up her own production firm when Mukerjea met her. To Mukerjea she seemed like a good choice given her experience in dealing with the government and the fact that she was not a journalist. He wanted someone who would figure out the tabloid part of the channel. Kohli joined Star News as president in April 2002. That was when the first cracks started to appear in a winning team.

'We were all executive vice presidents, she came in as president. To soothe feathers Sameer was made COO. But the way it was handled left a bad taste. It was not about who made it; at that time everybody was deserving. It was not discussed, not told. So I decided to leave,' says Nayak. He later took up the NDTV offer to head their news business. This became the cause of litigation between Star and Nayak since there was a non-compete clause in his contract. 'Peter brought Ravina [in] as a foil. That upset Sameer and Raj. Raj wanted the Star News job. From then on the rift started. On the executive floor, there was a wall between Peter and Sameer,' says Sumantra Dutta, who was heading Radio City.

To this undercurrent of conflict add a few other factors.

Star News had taken off. Kohli had done a good job getting the tone and tenor of the channel right. With shows such as *Vir Ke Teer*, an hour-long show that took a look at the story behind a big news break, and *Masand Ki Pasand*, with film critic Rajeev Masand, Star News was getting the right mix of high-quality, non-serious journalism. Television critics, especially media writers, sneered at it as another example of Murdoch's tendency to dumb down.

But this was a different market. In February 1998, when Star News first launched, there was no twenty-four-hour news channel— now there were more than half a dozen. (In fact, India currently has a staggering 400-plus news channels, most of them appallingly compromised or plain terrible.) Before she relaunched Star News, Kohli went to almost every major News Corp market to understand how news worked, the technology used, what clicked. Soon Star News started creeping up the ratings chart in Aaj Tak's strongest market, Uttar Pradesh. Within a few weeks of its launch, it became the No. 2 in Hindi news.

Remember that around the time it was launched, Star News had changed hands thanks to the revised uplink norms issued late in 2003, which decreed that 51 per cent equity in a news channel should be held by an Indian entity. (See Chapter 7, 'The Making of India's Largest Media Company'.) ABP Group came in with a

74 per cent shareholding in MCCS, the joint venture that ran Star News. Aveek Sarkar, the editor-in-chief and part-owner of ABP, is a character in his own right. He has a fine editorial mind and probably had his own ideas on what the channel should be about. In February 2004 Star News hired Uday Shankar as editor and director of news. Shankar had been news director of Aaj Tak and the man credited in large part with its success. Clearly, Star News was planning to change direction. By August 2004 Kohli quit and Shankar became CEO of MCCS. Later, he went on to become president of the Asia business and chairman and CEO of Star India. (His story follows in the next chapter.)

By 2004 it was becoming evident that Star was too dependent on Star Plus. It was the be-all and end-all of what Star had to offer. Star India had eighteen channels and *Kyunki Saas Bhi Kabhi Bahu Thi* was still the most popular show on TV. *KBC*'s second season broke Indian viewership records in its debut episode. Still, it was the same channel, the same shows, the same team and the same network that was delivering all of this. Where was the diversification, the other revenue streams? There was Star Vijay, a Tamil channel Star had acquired at some point from UTV; there was the stake in Hathway, the joint venture with ESPN and radio. There was no regional bouquet like Zee's or an international business that could leverage existing content.

These were the questions I asked Mukerjea several times in the years I knew him. I never got a clear answer. 'I don't think there is a risk involved with being dependent on broadcasting because it is not a saturated market. There is, however, a risk involved with being dependent on Star Plus. That is why it is important for us to strive for leadership in all those categories we are in, whether it is English movies, music or sports or news,' said Mukerjea. Star did launch more Hindi channels. Star One came in 2004 with the intention of keeping the audience for high-end Hindi entertainment within the Star fold. It entered the list of top fifty shows very quickly with *The Great Indian Laughter Challenge* and *Nach Baliye*, a dance show. In the same year, Star Utsav went on-air with the library programming of Star Plus. The idea was to get people to convert to cable TV in small-town India. Still, Star Plus and Balaji Telefilms continued to bring in a chunk of Star's audience and revenues. In August 2004 Star bought a 26 per cent stake in Balaji for Rs 150 crore ($34 million). 'They bought into me because I was erratic and they were scared,' says Kapoor with trademark directness. Kapoor was—and remains—one of the most temperamental stars in the Indian content business.

You could argue that just keeping up with a market that was growing at a scorching pace and being at the top was a full-time job. It was. Star Plus's hegemony over prime time was challenged several times, usually by Sony. For example, at some point in 2001–2002, two Sony shows, *Kkusum* and *Kutumb*, started taking viewership away from Star Plus in the 9–10 p.m. slot. It took a year, but Star finally beat those programmes with weekly, one-hour shows instead of dailies. That was how big hits such as *Sanjivani, Des Mein Niklla Hoga Chand* and *Kehta Hai Dil* were born. 'Once you get to No. 1 the issue of staying there becomes critical. To try and expect another surge would be extremely optimistic. Growth will happen but in short sharp bursts rather than in a major push,' said Mukerjea. 'Even as we diversified [into Vijay TV, DTH, Star Gold] the dependence on Star Plus was huge . . . it is the stupendous success of Star Plus that allowed for everything else to happen,' says Nair.

But Star was fighting too many tactical battles and spending more and more to maintain its dominance over prime time. It needed a grand strategy to grow beyond Hindi TV. There was Radio City, but the market didn't have scale. The total market size was about Rs 100 crore ($21 million) in ad revenues when Radio City was launched. After Radio City and many of the other private players came in, this went up to Rs 360 crore ($82 million) in 2005. [Even today, radio is a Rs 3100 crore ($450 million) business, or about 1.8 per cent of the media and entertainment industry.] However much it grew, radio could never provide the scale that TV, or say DTH, could.

The big bet on DTH

Luckily, DTH had been revived since the ban was lifted late in 2000, the year that Star had turned around. The government had set stringent norms on foreign equity and a broadcaster could not own more than 20 per cent in a DTH company (it still can't). Star applied for a DTH licence in October 2002. However, it was Zee that got permission first and launched in 2003. This time too, just as in 1996, Star was kept waiting for a long time.

Meanwhile, in January 2004, Star signed a joint venture agreement with Tata Sons for a DTH project. Tata Sons would hold 80 per cent in Space TV, the working name of the venture, while Star Group would hold the rest. Ishaat Hussain, then finance director of Tata Group, became chairman of Space TV. Hussain, who is acknowledged as one of India's finest managers, retired from Tata Group in 2017 after thirty-six years. The Tatas, represented by Hussain, were (and still are) wise allies going by the account of senior managers. (Hussain did not respond to my request for an interview.)

Vikram Kaushik, then vice president at food giant Britannia Industries, was hired as CEO. His first job was to get the DTH licence, a task that took almost two years even after the joint venture agreement had been signed. While Kaushik doesn't say it, almost every senior manager in the Star system knew that the government was miffed with Star's back-door entry into radio and was holding out on the DTH licence. 'We were told that if we got out of radio we would get the DTH licence,' says a very senior manager from that time.

Star relented. In January 2005, Music Broadcast, Radio City's holding company, was sold to India Value Fund, a private equity firm. That was when the government decided that Star was serious about not trying to bend the rules. In May 2005, Space TV got its licence. By July it had changed its name to Tata Sky. The guidelines did not allow a broadcaster to own more than 20 per cent in DTH. And this time, Star stuck to the guidelines, though rivals Zee and

Sun continue to own a majority stake in their DTH businesses through subsidiaries or associate companies. Even DD, the state broadcaster, has a fully owned DTH operation.

Star gave up radio to become a minority partner in a business where it brought in all the knowledge of running some of the largest DTH brands around the world. But News Corp and New York were happy. Vikram Mehra, currently the CEO of Saregama, who joined Tata Sky as vice president sales and marketing in 2001, went through the whole process of trying to get permission and putting together the business plan even when it seemed that nothing was happening. Note that for Star, this was the second time within five years that it was attempting to set up a DTH business. Mehra remembers being surprised by the 'perseverance of the system once it decided that it will go after something'.

After more than a decade of trying, a $33 million write-down in 1999 and relentless opposition, Murdoch was finally looking at launching a DTH brand in India. By the time Kaushik came on board, a lot of work had gone into the DTH plan. Mehra had gone to News Corp–owned DTH firms in Chile, Brazil, the UK and Australia to figure out the business. He made multiple presentations to both Murdoch and James (till the latter was in Asia). 'The only thing they said was "think big, don't save pennies",' he recalls. 'News Corp was at only 20 per cent [share] but it pushed us to use the best technology, gave people, time and resources. At one time there were more than forty expats in our office,' says Kaushik. He asked Hussain why they had asked him to come on board. Hussain's answer: because Kaushik was a consumer goods person and the Tatas wanted him to create and define the category with what would eventually be known as Tata Sky.

'Cable was commoditized; it had infrastructural constraints and was completely in the informal sector. Everything was in cash and undeclared. Branded DTH was an idea whose time had come,' remembers Kaushik. Inspiration also came from mobile telephony, which was going through the roof. India had hit 165 million mobile connections by 2006, the bulk of them prepaid. In a poor country, people preferred small recharges and did not want to be shocked with a big bill later. That, for Kaushik, was a big lesson for DTH. In August 2006, Tata Sky was launched as a prepaid service.

'We came two-three years after DishTV. Theirs was a low-cost offering and they went for cable-dark markets. We said we will sell packages, prepaid, high-end, interactive and do kids/education. Tata Sky's average revenue per user is at a premium and churn is the lowest. We learnt from Sky UK and from Foxtel [Australia],' says Kaushik. Tata Sky has a better hold over the higher end of the market with Rs 5720 crore ($893 million) in revenues from just over 15 million subscribers in the year ending March 2018. The Rs 4637 crore ($724 million) DishTV, Zee's sibling, is the largest private DTH operator with 23 million subscribers in the same period.

Tata Sky is now among India's top ten media firms and a cash machine par excellence because of the prepaid model. Though 21st Century Fox owns only 20 per cent of it directly (and 10 per cent indirectly), Tata Sky has arguably turned out to be the only happy joint venture Star has had in the Indian market. Its launch in 2006, however, was one of the toughest that Star has had, for two reasons.

One, the cable environment was openly hostile to any new way of selling TV signals, especially one that brought transparency. A few days before the launch, a man in pyjama and kurta, bearing a scar, entered Kaushik's office at Star House in Worli and placed a pistol on his desk. '"You can't come to our area", he told me. I said it is a new technology, available all over the country, you can't stop it,' says Kaushik. The next day, fourteen Tata Sky employees in Kharghar, a town on the outskirts of Mumbai, were beaten up and had to be hospitalized.

The second, bigger reason was the atmosphere at Star India.

Star versus Star

Late in 2003, soon after James left, Michelle Guthrie, a lawyer who had worked for News Corp in London and Australia for over a decade, was brought in as Star Group (Asia) CEO. Guthrie was an insider but not an owner-manager in the way James was. She was also, apparently, an abrasive and bottom-line-oriented CEO. (Guthrie did not respond to my request for an interview.) 'Star made errors under Guthrie. There was unnecessary conflict with India and too much focus on EBITDA [earnings before interest, taxes, depreciation and amortization],' says one middle manager from that time. It is something almost everyone on the executive team from 2003 onwards reiterates.

Maybe Guthrie wasn't to blame. Hong Kong had no work on hand except to monitor India. In 2005, Star India brought in 67 per cent of the group's Asian revenues, all the profits in the region, 1 per cent of its global revenues and 11 per cent of operating income growth. A report from Merrill Lynch, New York, in October 2005 touted Star India as the only financial driver for News Corp's Asian business in the 'foreseeable future'. Jessica Reif Cohen, an analyst with Merrill Lynch, New York, valued it at $3 billion in a report at that time.

No other market was delivering anything of significance. When Guthrie came on board there was still hope from China. In 1999, when Murdoch married Wendi Deng, a thirty-year-old intern at Star TV's Hong Kong office, the rumour mills said that the marriage was Murdoch's gambit to crack the China market. That may not be true—the marriage lasted till 2013, long after Murdoch gave up on the China dream. In any case Deng was a key associate in building bridges with China, getting access, meeting people. Yet China did not deliver. At some point in 2007 an exhausted News Corp just gave up and decided to focus all its energies on India, around the time when Tata Sky was being launched. There was talk of shifting the head office to India. The only reason Hong Kong existed was because it was the regional uplink hub. Since policy had been liberalized in India, Star could have easily uplinked all its channels out of India. Hong Kong had nothing to do but 'sit on our heads', grumbles one former manager.

'We had a very difficult time while launching because of Michelle. Everything was governed by what Hong Kong said,' says a former senior manager from Tata Sky. This included colours, logos and other brand material. India didn't need this help—it had perfectly capable managers, many of whom were ready for the next big thing: a push overseas, heading a new project. The top of the pyramid was already too small to accommodate all the talent Star had stockpiled. In the booming Indian market where opportunities were aplenty, several people left—Rajesh Kamat went to head Endemol, Tarun Katial went to Sony, Tony D'Silva left to head the DTH venture for Sun TV. Many industry observers had been speculating on whether Mukerjea would be rewarded with a Hong Kong or New York posting after James left; no such opportunity came his way.

'I have been CEO since 1999, for seven years now. But the Indian market is not a mature, saturated one. So I want to stay and do things here. If you talk to a regular Indian executive they think that an overseas posting is good. I studied and worked overseas for eighteen years and made a conscious decision to return to India from London. Why would I go back to a 2-per-cent-a-year-growth economy?' Mukerjea retorted to my question about why he was still in India in 2006.

There were several talented executives who were creating an inexorable push upwards that was turning Mukerjea's seat wobbly. By early 2005 it looked like Mukerjea was losing to both Hong Kong and Nair. Nair's youth, closeness to Hong Kong and programming acumen (Star's biggest strength) worked against Mukerjea, who was seen as the ad sales guy who made it big, say many. Also, Guthrie's bottom-line orientation meant that any proposal for diversification—pushing into south India, for example—was shot down. 'Peter never got support from New York on regional channels. Vijay [Star's Tamil channel] was consuming too much management time with very little gain to show for it. K.D. [Kaushal Dalal], Sameer [Nair], Peter and I were the single biggest proponents for going regional,' says Ajay Vidyasagar, who was then president, Star India. Amongst other things he had been vice president and head of regional channels in 2001 and had run Star Vijay for a while. Vidyasagar went on to become regional director, Asia-Pacific, YouTube and Google. 'Peter and me worked very well together. After Michelle's coming territorial disputes started. Peter wanted to expand outward, Michelle said no and he started looking inward,' says Nair.

Mukerjea apparently had trouble getting along with Guthrie. Coming as she did in place of James, comparisons were inevitable. Almost every manager who has worked with him says this unequivocally: James leaves you alone. He might disagree on a decision but would always say, 'That is what I think, the decision is yours.' Mukerjea and James were both young when Star was down in the dumps. Mukerjea had just become CEO and James chairman when they started to rebuild it together. There was a bond there, a trust that was not easy to replicate. Much later, when Mukerjea was no longer at Star, he continued to be friends with James, meeting him for lunch on visits to London. In the summer of 2006 when I asked him if Guthrie interfered too much, Mukerjea's 'no comment' was telling.

When 2006 rolled in, things were falling apart at Star. The jostling between Nair and Mukerjea, between Hong Kong and India, had created two camps. People from one camp couldn't stand those in the other, even in the elevator, says one old-timer. In March 2006 Star India was split into two units—Star Group and Star Entertainment. Mukerjea became the CEO for Star Group. He was responsible for all corporate functions such as legal, finance, government affairs and corporate communications. He also managed Star's investments such as Tata Sky, Hathway, Balaji and MCCS, and was responsible for developing new business opportunities in India. He continued to report to Guthrie. Nair's regional boss, Steve Askew, the COO, became president of Star Entertainment. Nair was promoted to CEO, Star Entertainment, India. His job was programming, marketing, advertising sales, and distribution and growth opportunities in new media including wireless and Internet. More importantly, he would report to Askew. Nair had won the battle for control of Star. And just like his predecessor Rathikant Basu in 1999, Mukerjea was sidelined. Life had come full circle.

The story did not end there, however. I met Mukerjea and Nair after the reorganization, for yet another cover story. Mukerjea spoke about the building of the outdoor business headed by Sumantra Dutta (who had launched Star's radio business), of gaming, merchandising and a whole lot of other revenue streams that could take Star beyond broadcasting. The idea was to get one-third of Star's top line from businesses other than TV. These could be mobile entertainment, Internet, outdoor, specialized magazines, licensed merchandising, home video and film studios. The plan was to build as diversified a media portfolio as possible over the next ten years.

The idea was right, but the timing and the man assigned to it were clearly wrong. Mukerjea had presided over the six best years of Star's existence in India. Six years is a long time to dominate any market, grow by double digits and have the steadiest team possible in the business. Star's share of audience was three times that of closest competitor Zee. It had outperformed the ad market and grown by 20–25 per cent (against Zee's 16 per cent). It was overdue for a bit of trouble.

This came when ratings began to soften throughout 2005 while the drama between Hong Kong and India was playing out. In cricket parlance, Star had taken its eye off the ball. Around this time, in October 2005, Zee TV launched *Saat Phere: Saloni Ka Safar*, a show about a dark girl's travails in colour-conscious India. Then it brought in *Kasamh Se* in January 2006. This was the story of three sisters who, after their father's death, have to live with his rich, ruthless businessmen friend. Both these came from a new team that was led by former Times Group president Pradeep Guha. Even as Zee crept up the charts Star was preoccupied shadow-boxing with itself. By December 2006 Zee was a clear, fresher No. 2. Its revenues were shooting up, so too was its stock price. Star's audience share continued to tumble. Worse still, it had to sell advertising inventory on *KBC 3* at a rate that was 25 per cent lower than for *KBC 2*. 'Star began to look faded. Peter and Sameer had no ideas beyond this on how to sustain,' says Kunal Dasgupta, who was then CEO of Sony.

The second quarter of 2006–2007 saw a drop of 36 per cent in operating income for Star India, going by an analyst call. This was the first contraction in profits since Star India started delivering profits in 2002.

Mayhem in Mumbai

All this was building up pressure inside the system. Something had to give—and when it did, it was in spectacular fashion. In a single fortnight in January almost all the CEOs quit—Guthrie, Mukerjea, Nair and Askew. Mukerjea was joining his (now former) wife Indrani's INX Global, which would go on to launch several entertainment channels. INX was funded by a clutch of investors who were backing Mukerjea, the man who had built Star India.[1] Nair was walking out to join NDTV Networks, which was starting Imagine TV, an entertainment channel, along with NBC Universal and Turner International. Steve Askew went on long leave. Paul Aiello, who had joined Star in Hong Kong in June 2006, took over as CEO in place of Guthrie. Aiello was the former managing director and head of the telecom, media and technology investment banking team for Morgan Stanley (Asia-Pacific). Many people left during this phase. Among them were Tony D'Silva (head of distribution), Gaurav Gandhi (vice president, commercial and business planning) and Shailaja Kejriwal (senior vice president and programming head).

---

[1] Peter Mukerjea was arrested in 2015 and is currently in jail awaiting trial. He is accused of being part of the conspiracy that led to the murder of Sheena Bora. His wife Indrani is accused of murdering Bora in 2012. Bora was her daughter from an earlier marriage, say news reports. Mukerjea has repeatedly claimed that he is not guilty. He and Indrani are also going through divorce proceedings. Almost the entire senior team that worked with Mukerjea has kept in touch with him, even going to meet him at court hearings. There is a WhatsApp group that updates participants on his court hearings. The affection he commands even now from his team is touching and telling.

Some went on to join Nair or Mukerjea, others to the dozens of companies waiting to welcome them.

'Sameer and Peter had done what had to be done. They couldn't reimagine Star. There was so much negative energy in such a successful company. After the blow-up in January–February 2007, Peter Chernin, then president and COO of News Corp, came and said things will be okay,' says a senior manager who quit soon after. All of us on the media beat knew that things were going terribly wrong at Star India. What on earth was New York doing when the one asset it had built in the region was blowing up in its face?

Part V

Uday Shankar (2007 onwards)

9

The Journalist CEO

A political reporter, small-town India, a divorce from Balaji and a marriage with Asianet

It was not a good beginning. Uday Shankar was the CEO of Star News when I first met him in June 2005 at the ITC Sonar Bangla hotel in Kolkata. Star News was (then) owned by Media Content and Communications Services or MCCS, a 74:26 joint venture between ABP Private Limited and Star India. I was associate editor at *Businessworld*, then an ABP magazine (it was subsequently sold). Shankar and I were, therefore, technically part of the same company. The occasion was the launch of Star Ananda, MCCS's second channel in Bangla. The managing director of ABP, Aniruddh Lahiri, introduced me as the resident media expert to Shankar. 'Yes. She spoke to me for half an hour and then used only one line,' Shankar responded.

Lahiri, who'd known me for a bit, joked that I should not take people who worked within the company for granted. That made me cringe. This is one of the perils of business journalism and the research it requires. We do several interviews but sometimes use only a few quotes from them—either because much of the material becomes background or because a story may be too short to use up all the quotes. This is what had happened in a story I did around the boom in news channels in September 2004. My telephonic interview with Shankar must have been just a month after he became CEO.

The moment passed. Shankar's name cropped up again. Once when Star News became No. 1 in August 2005 and later with its coverage of both local and national issues. It was not exactly NDTV but it wasn't the tabloid channel that Peter Mukerjea, CEO, Star India, and Ravina Raj Kohli, the founding president of Star News, had envisaged when it was launched in 2003. This was a Star News that had a character and tone that was distinct from anything else in the market. At an ABP meet in Delhi I complimented Shankar on the work the news team was doing. Still, when he became COO of Star India in April 2007 and later CEO in October, I was as surprised and sceptical as most. Sure, he had created Aaj Tak and run MCCS but he was a political reporter and a star editor and had become a good CEO, albeit of a news company. Could he run a Rs 1600 crore (just over $400 million) entertainment company that was floundering? The bets were that he would not last long.

Shankar proved everyone wrong, and spectacularly so. Under him, Star has grown more than eight times to become a Rs 13,448 crore ($2.06 billion) company. It is now a leading player across entertainment, sports and films. It is India's largest media conglomerate, along with the Zee Group. It now owns Hotstar among the three largest OTT brands from India along with YouTube India and MX Player; gets about a fourth of its top line from non-Hindi broadcasting; and owns the rights to every major sports event there is. On the way it has created some programming that is truly unique—for example, the Pro Kabaddi League that revived a rustic Indian sport in stunning fashion. (More on this in Chapter 11, 'The Star That Shankar Made.')

Shankar's biggest contribution, to my mind, is that he has managed to take more than a decade of resentment about Star's foreign origins and turn that around so that a lot of people now think of it as an Indian company. 'We are now on our second generation of local management and an entirely local leadership team. We don't have expats that come in and run the business; it's entirely local, entirely. Star is an Indian business,' emphasized Joseph Nallen, chief financial officer, 21CF, in a Deutsche Bank media, Internet and telecom conference in 2016. After more than a decade at the helm, 'He is Star. His and Star's name is intertwined,' reckons Deepak Jacob, president and general counsel, Star India. 'It is Uday's company in DNA, not ownership. They [the Murdochs] like him because he is what they are,' says Ajit Thakur, who worked at Star as executive vice president for three of its channels from 2011 to 2015. Shankar dominates every aspect of its business, every major decision it makes, perhaps more so than Mukerjea, who was very hands-off.

Shankar and Mukerjea do have one factor in common when it comes to their success—James Murdoch. Even while Shankar was struggling to figure out how to tackle the mess he had inherited, James was appointed chairman and CEO of News Corporation for Europe, Asia and the Middle East in December 2007. This made him the big boss for the India market. In mid-2009, Shankar started reporting directly to James. This gave Shankar the same corporate backbone in the head office that Mukerjea had had. Just like Mukerjea and James made magic along with the Indian management team, the combination of Shankar and James has catapulted Star into a $2 billion company that every analyst in New York now discusses on every earnings call with the management of 21st Century Fox (News Corp was spun into two firms in 2013.) In the middle of 2018 when Disney bought out Star's parent 21st Century Fox in a $71.3 billion deal, Star India was valued at anywhere between $10–15 billion against $3 billion in 2005. By the time you read this book, Star would have become a Disney company.

But that happened much later. This part of Star's story begins with Shankar and the mess he had inherited.

The other Peter

'In 1991, when the Gulf War happened, I went to a friend's place in west Delhi to watch it on CNN. We had drinks and dinner and we watched the power of journalism and the power of TV. It was love at first sight. This combination of TV plus journalism was my epiphany, I was just out of journalism school [Times School of Journalism],' remembers Shankar. The Bihari twang in his accent is evident only if you are Indian and have strained to understand which part of the country a fellow Indian is from. After a master's in economic history from Jawaharlal Nehru University, Delhi, Shankar did a postgraduate diploma in journalism before going to work for the *Times of India*, Patna. The Sahara Group, Zee and even an environment magazine, *Down to Earth*, followed. He'd worked briefly at the India Today Group when it was producing Aaj Tak as a news bulletin for Doordarshan. When NDTV's Prannoy Roy shifted to Star News from Doordarshan, the TV division of the India Today Group got the contract to cover the 1998 elections for the public broadcaster. Aroon Purie, publisher and chief editor of the group, then asked Shankar to work on the 1998 elections. Later, when Aaj Tak was being launched as a new channel, Shankar was hired. That was his big break.

At age thirty-eight, Shankar became news director for Aaj Tak, TV Today's Hindi news channel, which was launched on 31 December 2000. Aaj Tak was an instant hit. By 2003, TV Today had gone public, and Shankar had launched a second channel, Headlines Today. He talks fondly of those days and recounts how several high-profile political leaders, starting with former (and late) prime minister Atal Bihari Vajpayee, loved watching Aaj Tak, and told him as much. News and journalism are topics he can discuss at length, and he has strong views on everything.

In 2003, there were about a dozen Hindi channels in the pipeline. NDTV was launching its own channels, and so were other broadcasters. The news market was bursting with action. Shankar joined Star News as editor and director of news in February 2004.

By August, Ravina Raj Kohli, the president of Star News, had left and Shankar was made CEO. That is when he started interacting closely with the team at Star House in Mumbai till he shifted to Delhi in 2006. He would meet Nair, Mukerjea and the whole team regularly and could see the company unravelling.

When the mess at Star resulted in four CEOs quitting in January 2007 (see Chapter 8, 'Star-crossed'), New York finally woke up. It deputed its best man, Peter Chernin, then president and COO of News Corp, to have a look at things. He now runs The Chernin Group, which invests and runs firms in media and technology. With Chernin's involvement, the search for a potential CEO began. Paul Aiello from the Hong Kong office had taken over as CEO of the Star Group in place of Guthrie early in 2007. When News Corp started looking for CEOs, one of the names that came up was Shankar. The senior team started checking on him. Much of the anecdote that follows is based on my chats with Shankar, for the book and otherwise. Both Aiello and Chernin declined to talk.

Soon after taking over, Aiello called Shankar, who was in Patna on a personal trip, to inform him that Mukerjea, Nair and Guthrie had quit. He wanted to meet Shankar. And they did meet, several times. It was a confusing time, people were quitting left, right and centre, and Aiello probably needed to make sense of things. He'd dealt with Shankar on the board of MCCS, so he was comfortable with him. Sometime in February, when Shankar was at a Star News offsite in Thailand, Aiello called again. Could he meet Peter Chernin, who was on a visit to Mumbai?

Shankar landed for the late afternoon meeting at the Grand Hyatt hotel near Mumbai airport. Later that night, he had a flight back home to Delhi. Chernin was on his BlackBerry for a bit before he turned around and asked Shankar what he thought had gone wrong with the India business. A tired, sleepy and somewhat impatient Shankar gave Chernin his unedited opinion on what had gone wrong and what needed to be done. 'There are four or five pools of content that work in India: news, drama, cricket, movies. You chose to play in one and it became more commoditized.

Anyone who has money can make a drama,' Shankar remembers telling Chernin. After about an hour, says Shankar, 'Chernin stated, "You are not saying that it cannot be fixed." I said, "Everything can be fixed."' They said their goodbyes and that was it. 'Paul [Aiello] was shaky about my outburst. I assumed the meeting had not gone well,' says Shankar.

However, the very next month, in March, Aiello called Shankar, who was in Patna once again. Could he come to Hong Kong this time? Aiello and Shankar had lunch at a Chinese restaurant on the first floor of the Harbour Plaza hotel next to the building that housed Star's regional headquarters. 'He said, "I would like you to work with us." I said, "I am." He said full time. So I said, "I am full time." That is when Paul said for Star India. I thought he wanted me to do content, so I asked him what he wanted me to do for Star India. He said, "We want you to run all of Star India as COO; I will be CEO,"' says Shankar, who was startled by the offer. Over lunch, Aiello and Shankar talked specifics. Shankar needed time to think. He had relocated to Delhi just six months back. He came back home and spoke to his wife, Anupama Shankar, who had worked briefly with Star. She reckoned the company was too messed up.

It was. In March 2007, Star Plus was hanging on to its leadership position by the skin of its teeth. Zee TV was already equal to Star Plus in audience share and looked like it would get ahead. The ratings of *KBC 3*, hosted by movie star Shah Rukh Khan, were in depressing single digits compared to the 15–20 that *KBC 2* had consistently enjoyed in 2005. *Kyunki* and *Kahaani* had gone through such ridiculous plot twists that even loyalists like me had stopped watching them. From 11 per cent in March 2006 the viewership share for all of Zee's channels had crept up to 15 per cent, marginally below Star's 16.2 per cent. Note that Star was never the No. 1 network in all those years; it was No. 2 after Sun TV with its awesome bouquet of channels in Tamil, Telugu, Malayalam and Kannada. Kalanithi Maran, the man who set up Sun TV, had not made any serious attempts, however, to bring his brand of programming and low ad rates to the north, so Star had continued to dominate that market, albeit with one product—Star Plus. Ad rates were falling, there was audience exhaustion and nobody was in charge. As one manager who joined in mid-2007 says, 'It was seen as a sinking ship. When I first walked into the office, it wore a desolate look.'

Paritosh Joshi, former head of revenue at Star India, remembers one review meeting in Mumbai in early 2008 where Chernin told the India team, 'Think of the India business as a skyline. There is one big Empire State building and nothing else. You and I are in a lopsided skyline with one Star Plus.' Joshi reckons, 'At that time the profit of Star India was more than that of Star Asia and the profit of Star Plus was more than that of Star India. What Chernin was saying was that a healthy business should have many sizeable contributors to the overall revenue and profitability. "At 20th Century Fox (News Corp's film studio), we don't depend on one *Avatar* or one *Titanic*, we fund a lot of independent and big-budget films," he said.'

The growth of small-town India

It was during this time that Murdoch travelled around India on an extended trip. This is what he wrote about his India travels in the 2008 annual report. 'Over July and August [2007], I spent a few weeks in Asia where I met some of our talented employees and was impressed by the hard work and growing self-confidence I saw throughout the region. In the historic city of Pune in western India, I saw plans to bring the Internet to the most remote of Indian villages. In Mumbai, I launched two Dow Jones indexes that will measure the rise of India's companies and its growing economy. Like the Chinese before them, the people of India suffered a grinding poverty that was caused by a failure of policy and was not a reflection of personal potential. But these inspiring individuals have picked themselves up and are determined to use their talents and skills to make a better life for themselves and their families. Their rise is to be celebrated and will surely provide our company with extraordinary opportunities in the future.'

Murdoch was commenting as someone who had been visiting India since the early 1990s. He had seen the changes that India had gone through from its media-dark, closed days to the happening economy of South Asia at the turn of the millennium. The opening up after 1991 meant so many things as the years went by. When I started my working life in 1992, in spite of a master's in management studies [or MBA] from a good institute, jobs were scarce and good jobs were scarcer still. You took what you got. By 2000, all of us with experience and a good degree were flooded with job offers, and by 2007 anyone well-educated in metro India had it made. By then, the Indian economy was growing at a scorching 9.4 per cent. Some of the bigger changes this was bringing about were evident—more consumers, more buying power and more media. There was the rise of digital media, radio, television; the making of India's first few multiplex chains and film studios had begun. Even organized retail was taking off with local chains like Shopper's Stop, Pantaloons and Big Bazaar.

Of all the changes taking place and therefore the opportunities that Murdoch talked of, two were critical.

The first was the rise of small-town India, something that Murdoch had alluded to in his letter. In purchasing power, time spent on media and product consumption, small-town India was seen as the next frontier of growth. 'The Dhoni Effect', a study by EY in 2007,[1] mapped affluence, population and growth potential in twenty-eight towns, including the six metros. The three-year trend in monthly household incomes across India showed that the steepest growth in the Rs 3000–Rs 10,000 bracket came from non-metros and rural areas. In terms of affluence, towns like Nasik, Indore, Vijaywada, Madurai and Chandigarh had reached three-fourths or more of the affluence levels of Mumbai. They made up the shortfall on that score in volumes since the number of affluent towns had been rising steadily.

---

[1]   While being employed by EY in 2007 I had led the research on this paper on small-town India. Later, EY did two more reports on the subject since there was phenomenal investment interest in the area.

On growth potential, they did even better. For example, telecom subscriber growth in the four metros was a scorching 57 per cent but in the rest of India it was even higher at 92 per cent, albeit on a lower base. For companies such as Hindustan Unilever, ITC and others, the push into small-town India began long before liberalization. They used events, video-on-wheels, radio, outdoor media and the regional editions of newspapers to reach consumers in small-town and rural India. Soon after economic liberalization began in 1991, the growth of consumer products, telecom and financial services that wanted to reach these prosperous small towns drove the phenomenal growth of newspapers in Hindi, Tamil and Telugu, among a dozen other languages.

The second change, therefore, was the texture of the Indian media market. Broadcasters had not yet fully tuned into small towns because TAM Media, the ratings agency, did not have a large enough sample beyond the big cities. Its rating numbers didn't reflect what residents of small towns were watching. To be fair to TAM, even if small-town viewership had been captured, media agencies (not advertisers) were usually disinterested. Over many years of covering media, I have commented on media planners' tendency to think and live in a Mumbai–Delhi ghetto of 'people like us'. In their English-speaking heads they have little idea about how strongly consumers connect to their local languages—irrespective of income or class. Even when Hindi, Marathi, Tamil and Bangla newspapers were bigger in circulation and readership than the English titles, the ad rates they attracted were as low as a fourth or a fifth of English. This was driven by the perception that anyone who didn't watch or read English is somehow a lesser consumer. It was popularly referred to as the 'English bias' or the 'premium on English', which had benefitted Star Plus for many years in the 1990s.

Post-liberalization, when the firms which owned some of India's biggest language dailies got in foreign investors, listed on the stock exchange and began actively marketing themselves is when the perception changed. Many of these firms—Jagran Prakashan, which publishes *Dainik Jagran*, one of the highest-selling newspapers in the world, or DB Corporation, which publishes the Hindi daily *Dainik Bhaskar*—have consistently delivered on profits. As the evidence of the growth in small towns, other languages and socio-economic classes piled up, marketers wanted to reach out to these consumers but planners were woefully ill-equipped. All they knew was how to put stuff into an optimizer (the software for media planning), which regurgitated the numbers and gave them a sense of where to put the client's money. English had traditionally been the language of the upper SECs (socio-economic classes). But now it was clear that Gujarati or Malayalam readers and viewers may be equal to if not better off than the upper-end English-speaking homes, going by the EY report. By 2007, the difference between the ad rates paid for an English- and Indian-language consumer was down to three times from four to five times pre-liberalization.

During the three years ending 2006, the number of people satellite TV reached grew at over 100 per cent in small-town India and over 200 per cent in rural India. Metro India, on the other hand, saw between 30–40 per cent growth in reach according to the Indian Readership Survey. By 2007, India had 117 million TV homes, more than 72 million of which were cable and satellite homes. There were hundreds of local cable channels offered by cable operators, most of who still cover an average of 500 to 1000 homes. Then there was the choice in languages other than Hindi. There was Zee with its regional bouquet, Sun TV with its phenomenal hold over all of south India, and Eenadu with its clutch of Telugu, Bangla, Urdu and other channels.

Star and Sony, however, had no regional business, nor were they even attempting to cater to the Hindi consumer in small towns. This was, in fact, a big part of Star's growth problem. If, two years ago, *Kyunki* and *Kahaani* had given a marketer reach across north and west India, in 2007, there were options in Marathi, Bangla and Punjabi pulling viewers and advertisers away. Since advertising was the single largest source of revenues that business plans hinged on, this was a critical trend to hitch on to. A bulk of broadcaster revenues came from the Rs 6000 crore ($1.4 billion) that advertisers spent on television in 2006. This dependence is true even today.

Shankar takes charge

It was against this background that two things happened.

One, Shankar took over as CEO by October 2007. He was forty-six then. Two, in July 2008, a TV channel called Colors was launched.

'Initially, Uday didn't do much. It was a period of learning and cleaning up house,' says Kunal Dasgupta, then CEO of Sony. 'When he [Shankar] came in, he questioned every status quo, pushed for breaking up the Balaji Telefilms arrangement and made lots of tactical and strategic moves. Uday [Shankar] is very aggressive and abrasive. A lot of people quit or complained to James. Jagdish [Kumar, former senior vice president, Star] and Sonali [Thakker, executive vice president], both old Star hands from the 1990s, became a bridge between the old and the new. Uday either likes you or he doesn't, and if he likes you, you will rise,' says one senior consultant who worked with Star during that phase.

Shankar says that when he walked into Star in 2007, the first challenge was convincing people. 'We had lost the plot and that we could regain it. I met the content team and told them, "I don't know anything about programming but as a journalist I have one skill—asking the right questions—and I will use that to solve this problem [of Star's falling popularity]," he told me in 2012 after Star had turned around.[2] This began by questioning existing beliefs. 'Within India and overseas there was an irrational belief that we couldn't exist without Balaji. The place was frozen, people were living in denial,' said Shankar.

The bad vibes between Balaji and Star were evident by then. In April 2007, just a little before Shankar joined, Star India had

---

[2]   In this portion, Shankar has been quoted largely from interviews done with him from 2010 onwards.

announced a 51:49 joint venture with Balaji Telefilms to launch channels in Telugu, Kannada and Malayalam, among other languages. The joint venture would also absorb Star Vijay, the firm's under-performing Tamil channel, and relaunch it. However, it never took off because Star didn't want to continue with Balaji.

'There has been a shift. Ten years ago, when Star Plus came out with shows like *KBC* and the Balaji series, they clicked with a certain kind of viewership universe. Television at that time was a big-city phenomenon. But as the cable and satellite universe grew, it went to Tier II cities, small towns and very small towns. It was easier for newer players to scan the environment and not be bogged down in legacy. That is what worked for our competitors and became a hurdle for us,' said Shankar in an interview to *Business Standard* in 2010.[3]

He was referring to Colors. Three new competitors had been spawned by Star. There was NDTV Networks, which was getting into general entertainment with Imagine TV headed by Sameer Nair, former CEO of Star. There was the bouquet of channels planned by INX Network, the firm that Mukerjea and his wife were running. And there was a new entertainment channel on its way from Viacom18. It was a 50:50 joint venture between Viacom and Raghav Bahl's Network18, then one of the most aggressive, fast-growing firms in the media and entertainment space.[4] Remember, it was the one that made the first ever show Star commissioned in India way back in 1993.

From a Rs 15 crore ($3.5 million) television production firm in 1999, Network18 had become a Rs 692 crore ($175 million) media conglomerate by 2007. It owned, among others, brands such as

---

[3] Suveen K. Sinha and Sharmistha Mukherjee, 'It Would Be Unfair to Blame Balaji: Q&A with Uday Shankar, CEO, Star India', *Business Standard*, 25 June 2010.

[4] Viacom18 is now majority owned by Reliance Industries which bought out the parent firm, Network18, in a complicated deal that started in 2012 and ended with Reliance taking control in 2014.

CNBC-TV18, HomeShop18, CNN-IBN and Moneycontrol.com. Colors, launched in July 2008, beat Mukerjea's 9X and NDTV's Imagine by several miles. More importantly, it beat both Star Plus and Zee to become the biggest Hindi entertainment channel within nine months of its launch. And it did this by using small-town, rural-oriented shows such as *Balika Vadhu* and *Tu Na Aana Is Des Meri Laado*. These shows took up issues like child marriage and the mad Indian fascination for having a boy child to build what were essentially kitchen politics shows in a different milieu. Then there was *Khatron Ke Khiladi*, the licensed Indian version of NBC's *Fear Factor*. The $14.63 billion Viacom was delighted. None of its earlier attempts in India—MTV, VH1, Nick or even Paramount Pictures—had seen this kind of success.

Incidentally, Colors was launched by another old Star hand, Rajesh Kamat, who had quit in 2006 to join Endemol India and then become the first CEO of Viacom18. Kamat, one of the brightest minds in the media business, joined Peter Chernins's The Chernin Group in 2011. He went on to become managing director of Emerald Media, a part of the US-based global investment firm KKR.

Colors's success incensed Shankar, say insiders. In October, it served Balaji with a termination notice on *Kyunki Saas Bhi Kabhi Bahu Thi*, by then one of the longest-running shows in India. It would be pulled off-air by November. An agreement between Star and Balaji stated that if the show's ratings fell below a certain figure, the channel was entitled to terminate the show. Between July and September 2008, *Kyunki*'s ratings fell by 32 per cent. Star went in for the kill. A showdown followed, with Balaji taking Star to court. 'They didn't get an interim relief or an injunction to stop us from launching another show. They lost before a single-judge bench, went in appeal to a two-judge bench and lost again. Then there was a settlement,' says Deepak Jacob, president and general counsel, Star India. 'Between 2008–10, the relationship with Star was very bad; I want to forget it,' is all that Ekta Kapoor, the creative brain and joint managing director of Balaji, has to say about that phase now.

Shankar was more circumspect in his analysis in a 2010 interview. 'In 1999–2000, when the relationship with Balaji Telefilms first began, there weren't many quality producers who were capable of delivering volumes. There were not many broadcasters who could finance the creative vision of Ekta. The cost of production was low; people wanted to do cheap shows. So it made sense for Star and Balaji to come together. They needed a buyer who could pay the premium to create content, and Star needed a supplier who could deliver quality content and volumes. There was a contract which was entered into—Balaji could not do prime-time programming for any other channel and Star could not offer prime-time slots to any other producer. There was an opportunity cost which was paid as a premium. As new broadcasters came in, the market opened up and there were more opportunities. Balaji felt, and rightly so, that it was being denied an opportunity to participate in the creative stream. Star felt that a whole new generation of producers and creative people had come into the market and because of the contract with Balaji they were being denied access. That was the real issue. This spilled over into issues over ratings and viewership. It was a mutual decision to free ourselves. Still, there has never been a quarter where we have gone without a Balaji show,' he said (see footnote 3).

This was classic Shankar—no-nonsense and ruthlessly clear. Much of the time it won him the admiration of people Star did business with.

Building the Indian language business

In August 2008, even while the Balaji storm was building up, Rupert Murdoch announced a Rs 42 crore ($8.6 million) investment in six Indian language channels. By November 2008, both Star Jalsha (Bangla) and Star Pravah (Marathi) were launched. Around the same time, Star started the process of buying Asianet Communications, a Bengaluru-based firm. It owned a bunch of popular channels in the south—Asianet, Asianet Plus (Malayalam), Suvarna (Kannada) and Sitara (Telugu), among others. Asianet was set up in 1991 by

Reji Menon and Sashi Kumar from Thiruvananthapuram, Kerala. It launched the first satellite channel in Malayalam in 1993 and became popular with audiences in India's most literate state. From 2003 onwards, Asianet started expanding into other geographies and languages. In 2006, Rajeev Chandrasekhar, who had made his money in consumer electronics and telecom (BPL), picked up a 51 per cent stake in Asianet Communications for an estimated Rs 150 crore ($33 million).

Chandrasekhar knew Shankar from his Aaj Tak days. So, when Asianet was looking for a majority investment, the two got talking. 'In India, mergers and acquisitions are minefields of traitorous commitments; I have been through it in telecom. When I walked into the deal I thought, "The big foreign company will ride roughshod over me." None of that happened. I never had to look behind my back for a knife being struck. Everything was upfront and candid, there was no drama. I had a twenty-minute conversation with Paul Aiello. There was no posturing. They wanted majority in two stages. I said we want to exit in the second stage because the valuation will go up. The deal happened within ten days,' remembers Chandrasekhar.

In January 2009, Star formed a joint venture with Chandrasekhar's Jupiter Entertainment Ventures, taking a 63 per cent share. Star Jupiter housed all general entertainment channels of Asianet Communications along with Star Vijay (Tamil). It paid approximately $235 million (Rs 1146 crore) in cash and assumed a net debt of approximately $20 million (Rs 98 crore) for a controlling interest in four of Asianet's channels.[5] Add to that Star Jalsha and Star Pravah, which had already been launched late in 2008.

---

[5] Going by News Corporation/21CF annual reports in July 2010, Star paid approximately $90 million (Rs 405 crore) in cash to increase its ownership stake to approximately 75 per cent. In fiscal 2013 it increased its interest to 87 per cent for approximately $160 million (Rs 992 crore) in cash. In May 2014 it acquired the remaining 13 per cent for approximately $50 million (Rs 295 crore) in cash.

However, its language portfolio could not be complete without Telugu, the language spoken in Andhra Pradesh (split in 2014 into two states, Andhra Pradesh and Telangana). Unified Andhra Pradesh is the state which makes the most films in India, has a whopping twenty news channels and is generally the most entertainment-crazy of the four southern states. Hyderabad, then a part of unified Andhra Pradesh, is a huge hub of film and TV content, just like Mumbai. In Andhra Pradesh, Maa TV, launched in 2002, had been on the rise for some time. In the last quarter of 2014 it overtook Sun's Gemini TV to become the leader. In February 2015, Star India entered into an agreement to acquire the broadcast business of Maa Television Network and its four Telugu channels for approximately $375 million (about Rs 2400 crore) in cash. This completed its portfolio in other Indian languages. The deal added about Rs 300 crore ($48 million) to Star's top line and about Rs 100 crore ($16 million) to its bottom line.

With Maa, Star had finally become a truly national network just like Subhash Chandra's Zee Entertainment and Reliance's Viacom18. By 2015 regional languages were driving more than 40 per cent of Star's profitability, according to one estimate.

For now we need to go back to 2008.

This was the time Shankar was putting together the team he wanted. By 2008, the Lehman crisis had happened, global markets were in a tailspin, and the valuation of Indian companies was in a downward spiral. The changes in the economy, competition and regulation meant the business challenges had become more diverse. 'The management team needed depth. Where could we get such a team from? There was no point in looking at other TV companies since most of them had people who had been with Star. There was no point in building a homogenous team when what we needed was diversity,' said Shankar in an interview later.[6] That is how Sanjay Gupta joined Star India as COO in April 2009. He became managing director in 2016.

---

[6]   This was in an interview with me for *Business Standard* in January 2010.

Gupta, the classic IIT–IIM (Indian Institute of Technology–Indian Institute of Management) type, was as different as possible from any of the senior managers Star had hired earlier. He'd been with Unilever for sixteen years and just before joining Star was the chief marketing officer of India's largest telecom firm then, Bharti Airtel. Gupta has turned out to be Shankar's best hire so far. Over the years, he's proved to be the right foil for him—bringing the operational chops while Shankar handles the outside world of government, New York and the big-picture dynamics, besides figuring out the content bit. In addition to Gupta, several other senior managers came in. There was Anupam Vasudev (from Hindustan Unilever who later left) and Amita Maheshwari, from MetLife India Insurance, who is president and head of HR. There were others who joined from businesses such as consumer products and banking.

'Instead of hiring creative people from production houses, we are going to campuses for creative talent. The television-viewing universe has expanded to include large, diverse markets from Uttar Pradesh to west Maharashtra to Bihar. Culturally, sociologically, these are different TGs [target groups]. Therefore, we need to look for diversity. We needed to stop hiring from the universe of Juhu–Versova [areas in north Mumbai that house major TV production firms and people who work for them],' said Shankar in the January 2010 interview.

But Star's struggles with Star Plus and Hindi were far from over. Shankar was pretty hands-on with programming in the first few years, by all accounts. Unlike Mukerjea, from concepts to producers to pilots, everything went through him. And his journalistic instincts were clearly at play going by the first few big shows that Shankar pushed for—*Aap Ki Kachehri* and *Sacch Ka Saamna*. *Aap Ki Kachehri* had a retired police officer, Kiran Bedi, adjudicating on disputes between parties at 10.30 p.m., prime time by Indian standards. It was not entertainment, and the characters it captured were not urban middle class. These were uneducated, poor people who wanted a solution to their problems. Given that it was not fiction, not drama and had none of the glamour of most reality shows, *Aap Ki Kachehri*, which launched in December 2008, did well. It garnered roughly half the viewership that the most popular show then, *Balika Vadhu* on Colors, got. It made it to the list of the top ten best-rated shows on Hindi entertainment channels and ran for three full seasons.

In July 2009 came *Sacch Ka Saamna*, a licensed version of *The Moment of Truth*. This one was tricky given that India is a conservative market and that television is a completely family medium. Before coming on the show, a contestant was asked fifty questions while being hooked to a polygraph machine. He was, however, not given the results. In the actual show, the contestant was asked twenty-one of the same questions again. If he answered honestly he could move to the next question. If he lied or refused to answer he lost all the money he had won. The questions got increasingly personal and ended up embarrassing the contestants. It raised a ruckus with several groups demanding it be pulled off-air since it was offensive, personal and culturally corrupting. 'Internally, we thought a lot about it [before launching the show]. We procrastinated for a long time. The real concern was whether our viewers would be turned off by the show, be outraged by it. We have a certain relationship of comfort with our viewers, especially with families and women who watch us. Were we going to risk that relationship? But the results of the show told us a very different story. The show had a lot of viewers and its unique reach was bigger than *KBC*,' said Shankar later in June 2010.

Much of this, however, didn't work at saving flagship Star Plus from plunging from No. 1 to No. 3 in the Hindi general entertainment channel sweepstakes. Colors and Zee continued to pummel Star in the largest, most valuable segment of the Indian TV market: Hindi general entertainment. As a network (with sixteen channels), though, Star remained ahead, second only to Sun TV.

Then came the biggest change, the one that gave Shankar wings. In June 2009, News Corp announced that India would replace Hong Kong as the regional head office. The Star channels would be uplinked from India instead of Hong Kong. Much of this ended up cutting about 200 jobs, including Aiello's. He quit by December that year. This meant that Shankar now reported directly to James, who was chairman and CEO for News Corporation Europe and Asia.

It was around this time that Star hired several research agencies to figure out consumers. 'We realized that our understanding of Indian society, which we capture in our shows, had to change. So, while the housewife is still committed to the family, she is a lot more assertive. She has material as well as emotional aspirations and she is not afraid to express them. The whole power equation in the family has changed. If we have to reclaim leadership, we would have to redefine ourselves,' said Shankar (see footnote 3).

The battle for the Hindi heartland

Vivek Bahl, now early-retired, was writing copy for one of India's largest ad agencies, Lintas, in 1990–91, when he got a call from Karuna Samtani, then head of production at Zee. She said Zee was being launched on the Star platform (See Chapter 1, 'Once Upon a Time . . .'); would Bahl be interested? Bahl joined Zee in mid-1992 as a programming executive three months before its October launch. He left in 1995 and then made shows on his own. Nine years later, he got another call from Zee and ended up joining as head of fiction in 2004, with Ashwini Yardi coming in as head of programming. (Yardi went on to head programming at Colors.) It is this combination of Bahl and Yardi that commissioned and made *Saat Phere*, *Ghar Ki Lakshmi Betiyaan* and *Banoo Main Teri Dulhan*, the shows that ensured that Zee bounced back in 2006. When Zee became successful, several broadcasters made overtures to Bahl. He met both Kunal Dasgupta of Sony and Ajay Vidyasagar, president of Star. 'I connected better with Ajay. I was doing mass content and didn't want to experiment with *Jassi Jaisi Koi Nahin* kind of content [the licensed version of *Ugly Betty* on Sony he had worked on before],' says Bahl. He joined Star as head of fiction programming for Star Plus and Star One in 2007 around the time Shankar came in.

'I had seen *Vivaah* [2006] and loved it. I wanted to make a series of it with some tweaks,' says Bahl. The Sooraj Barjatya film, released in 2006, was a blockbuster which did very well in small-town India. It is about a small-town girl who is brought up by her uncle who loves her. However, her aunt resents her since she is better looking than their own daughter and has therefore better prospects in fairness- and marriage-obsessed India. What Bahl had in mind was the story of a good-looking girl who is dogged by ill-luck. Sooraj Barjatya is a part of the Barjatya family that owns one of the oldest and most conservative studios in India, Rajshri Productions. It has also produced some of the biggest hits Indian cinema has ever seen, *Hum Aapke Hain Kaun* (1994) and *Maine Pyaar Kiya* (1989) among them.

Bahl approached Rajshri and they began working on it. The casting and scripting was done when Barjatya reportedly told Bahl that he wasn't happy with the script and wanted a few months more to rework it. 'It was my first show at Star, we were like six weeks from the launch. Star had already given notice to shut the other show in the 9 p.m. slot. I panicked,' recalls Bahl. He requested Rajshri to let him make it with another producer and they agreed. 'I made sure they were paid for the concept and their credit was carried throughout the run of the show,' says Bahl.

It was around this time that Rajan Shahi, who had directed two hits on Zee—*Saat Phere* and *Ghar Ki Lakshmi Betiyaan*—was itching to set up shop on his own. Zee was and still is one of the most bottom-line-focused media firms in India. 'At Zee, we always looked for a new producer because the costs would be lower. So I had never worked with Balaji [a high-end producer by then],' says Bahl. That is how Bahl turned to Shahi instead of an established production house. He asked Shahi if he was ready to turn producer and Shahi said yes. But he was an unknown quantity. Bahl introduced Shahi to Shankar and recommended that they get him to produce a show for Star. Given Star's unhappiness with Balaji's ageing and expensive

shows, this fit into its plans. Shankar agreed and *Sapna Babul Ka . . .
Bidaai* was launched in October 2007.

Shahi's production house Director's Kut was launched with
Sapna Babul Ka . . . Bidaai. 'Star Plus was very used to big sets
and jewellery. *Bidaai* was a simple show about a girl next door.
That was the big gamble. It broke the trend of the camera doing
the acting, bringing more real actors and new faces to television,'
says Shahi. He is referring to the sweeping camera movements and
loud background music that had become standard fare on Balaji's
and other soaps. Nobody expected much from *Bidaai*. This was
Star's down-and-out phase, and here it was, betting on an unknown
producer. The entertainment press was derisive. *Bidaai* became the
most-watched show in India within three months and ran for three
years. It averaged a rating of 5 and on good days hit 7. The days of
a 10 or 15 rating were long gone.

Shahi started getting the special treatment that Shankar is
famous for giving key associates. He spent time understanding and
discussing the issues around India's overcrowded, overworked and
cut-throat TV production business with Shahi. The system then was
the producer sent the episode of the day to the broadcaster, living
from episode to episode. 'We were all burning ourselves out, the
shows were looking the same and nobody had time to spend on
scripting. And if ratings went down, there were knee-jerk reactions.
He [Shankar] said don't change [the storyline just because ratings
are going down],' says Shahi. This was the journalist in him
telling the creator to stick to their vision. In fact, he insisted that
the programming team give all the feedback to Shahi and call him
for focus groups and promo meetings to ensure there was the least
possible information loss from broadcaster to content creator.

This was very unusual, and still is, in the Indian TV content
ecosystem. The bulk—maybe more than 80 per cent—of all the
programming on India's 800-plus TV channels is commissioned
by broadcasters who then own the intellectual property or IP in
perpetuity. The content business in India is an exhausting, dog-eat-
dog world. For a broadcaster to ask his firm to put a producer—who

is treated like a lowly vendor—in the feedback loop was unusual. Shahi attended a series of workshops on screenplay writing, looked at research and went through all that Star wanted him to.

By 2008, there was talk of doing another show with Shahi, this one about a young couple's journey in an arranged marriage. *Yeh Rishta Kya Kehlata Hai* went on-air in January 2009, getting in a rating of 5.6 from the word go. 'During that phase both *Bidaai* and *Yeh Rishta* were No. 1 and 2 alternately,' remembers Shahi. *Bidaai* was pulled off-air at its peak in November 2010. 'Uday decided to do that because it was at its peak and there was no need to do gimmicks and keep it running,' says Shahi. Star had made the mistake of keeping *Kyunki* and *Kahaani* on-air long after they were exhausted as stories; it didn't want to repeat that. 'The biggest risk in a business is an aversion to risk. In Hindi, the shows we were running had run out of life. But we did not show enough courage and change the formula when it was working best. If we had done that we could have avoided some of the mess,' said Shankar later.

In 2009 came *Mann Ki Awaaz Pratigya*, the story of the educated, courageous daughter of a professor from Allahabad. The son of a local landlord (and a goon) falls for her and is obsessive in his attempts to marry her. She decides to marry into his family in order to fix things. 'Since the Balaji arrangement ended [in 2008] we have started recreating the channel slot by slot. We have picked the largest number of new producers, some of their shows work, some don't. But we have started creating shows with distinct sets of viewers in mind—upmarket, small towns. We need to look at the channel [Star Plus] as a bunch of channels, like newspapers do it with sections,' Shankar said to me in 2010.

By 2010, Star had regained its mojo enough to go out and talk to everyone about what it was doing. Star Plus was firmly No. 1 once again. In June 2010, Star Plus marked the completion of a decade of being Hindi with a new look and programming. At a huge event with the who's who of media in attendance, it unveiled a new logo, designed by Venture 3, a London-based brand solutions firm.

Its new tagline said, 'Rishta wohi soch nayi', meaning 'The same relationship with new thinking'.

Colors's taking over the top slot had underlined that Star was mortal after all. For Shankar, the first challenge was to get the operation back on track. 'He brought Star Plus back in the reckoning. A lot of the credit for that goes to his content mind,' says Raghav Bahl, former head of Network18 and now co-founder, Quintillion Media. Most of his producers and writers agree. 'Once, I was agonized about the plot of *Yeh Rishta Kya Kehlata Hai*. Akshara [the protagonist] had got married and I was stuck. Around that time I had a meeting with Uday and told him about it. So he said, "Why are you worried? I see her son going to college. It is an evergreen story. You need to settle after a peak before you get on to another peak,"' remembers Shahi.

Around this time, Bahl brought another new producer on the Star radar. Sumeet Mittal was a freelance writer on successful shows such as Sony's *Ek Mahal Ho Sapno Ka*. He'd worked with Rajshri Productions on several TV shows and a film, *Ek Vivaah Aisa Bhi*, as assistant director. He'd known Bahl from his Zee days. 'When Bahl joined Star he said you make a show, produce it. It was their confidence that helped me to start producing,' says Mittal. That is how Mittal formed Shashi–Sumeet with his wife. The firm has done twenty-eight shows since then, seven of them for Star. 'As a writer, everything I did was on paper. But with Star, whatever I conceived came on the screen,' says Mittal. The first show he made for Star Plus, *Diyaa Aur Baati Hum*, in 2011, became a massive hit, bringing Star back in the reckoning. The story of a young woman whose dream of being an IPS officer is nurtured and pushed towards fulfilment by her traditional husband and in-laws found resonance with many ordinary women struggling within the confines of their social mores.

Star Plus was back at the top. And Star was once again leader in the one genre that brought it its bread, butter and jam: Hindi general entertainment.

10

Star Sports a New Look

Aamir Khan, cricket, push for pay and friendship with Zee

By 2011, Star was on a roll. The share of audience for its network of (then) thirty-three channels had grown from 13 per cent in 2008 to an unassailable 19.5 per cent by the beginning of that year. This meant that Star's channels accounted for about a fifth of all TV viewing in India. From Rs 1600 crore ($400 million) in June 2006, revenues had more than doubled to Rs 3652 crore ($562 million) in March 2011.[1] It was once again the largest broadcast network

[1] Till the financial year 2009, Star India's revenues were according to its financial year, which is July–June. Though its financial year remains the same, from 2010 the figures in this book have been presented according to the Indian financial year, which is April–March. This is because Media Partners Asia has shared the data in that format. Also, over these years, the conversion is at Rs 65 to the dollar. Media Partners Asia uses a constant exchange rate for historical financials that reflects a reasonable average over these years.

in India on both revenue and audience share. Its new channel, Life OK, was a huge success on the back of shows such as *Devon Ke Dev . . . Mahadev* and *Savdhaan: India Fights Back*. Life OK, which replaced Star One in 2011, was born out of research into viewing habits which showed a gap in the Hindi-speaking market.[2] Its non-Hindi broadcast business brought in 27 per cent of revenues (and profits), against 5 per cent in 2008 when it had embarked on building other languages.

Shankar had cut through the clutter, making a break from partnerships and joint ventures that did not serve either a strategic or a tactical purpose. The stakes in Balaji, Hathway, MCCS (Star News) and ESPN were all either being scrutinized or on the block. 'We got into the JVs not because we wanted to be a financial investor in the business but because we wanted to partner in building a business. However, if because of the partner's point of view or because of regulation we cannot do that, then it is better to exit,' he said to me in 2012. For instance, in MCCS, regulation stopped Star, as a foreign company, from upping its stake over 26 per cent or getting more involved in the editorial. 'Besides attending board meetings, there was nothing we could do,' he reckoned. It waited very long for the foreign investment limits in news to be pushed up to 51 per cent before giving up. By June 2012, News Corp sold its stake in Star News, one of Murdoch's favourite projects. It is now ABP News.

A very fundamental transformation of Star was in progress by 2011–12—from a one-channel wonder to a proper media conglomerate. The most important part of the transformation was its changed approach to programming in the mature Hindi market. 'Star understood the big-city viewer very well. But as cable and satellite TV went deeper, the understanding of that viewer had to improve,' says Shankar. The 2010 'Rishta wahi soch nayi' campaign along with new shows aimed at small towns worked, albeit slowly. There was no single programme which signified the 'new, improved' Star in bright neon signs the way *KBC* had done for Star in 2000.

---

2   It was rebranded Star Bharat in 2017.

Shankar is a man of strong opinions. And, like many journalists, he is not afraid of voicing them. Also, as anyone who has worked with or observed him will tell you, he is wedded to his opinions. In private conversations, he is scathing in his observations about the big issues in India or about the state of the media. In his JNU days, he leaned left, like most graduates from that iconic university do. My bet is that corporate life has smoothed the rough edges. However, his interest, his mindset was one of a journalist in the old mould—he wanted the media to give back to society. It was all fine to make Star the No. 1 channel with *Bidaai* or *Yeh Rishta* . . . but it was probably not fulfilling enough. Vivek Bahl, who joined as head of fiction programming in 2007, says that Shankar gave him a free hand with fiction programming. But Shankar mentioned that he believed the future of general entertainment content would largely be driven by non-fiction.

That is probably where his heart was. It was an interesting situation. He had got the company back on track and had the backing of the scion of the Murdoch family. 'They are very aggressive investors; Murdoch opens the chequebook easily. What everybody underestimates is the backing of the Murdochs, too much credit goes to the CEOs,' says Raghav Bahl.

As one former manager from the Mukerjea team puts it: 'After Paul left, Uday was reporting straight to the Murdochs. He got a free hand. The aggression came because there was backing and capital. Half of Uday's success is managing James, getting him aligned.' Note that James was also, probably, more invested in Star than many of the other businesses he handled; it was where he had cut his teeth. 'When James came back he decided to double down on India. He said we should spend our capital where there is ingrained local talent and the ability to grow scale, and he recognized that he had in Uday Shankar a catalyst to drive future growth,' says Vivek Couto. So there was a sense of 'let the India team do whatever it takes to move the business to the next level'.

In many ways, then, 2012 was when Shankar moved in for the kill. Some of the biggest investments Star made—in programming, acquisitions, new businesses and other media—were seeded or begun in that year. He also put in effort and time to sort out issues that would help weed out ancient obstacles that were holding back the growth of the world's second-largest TV market. For instance, the logjam in cable and therefore pay revenues (discussed below) or the lack of a robust measurement metric. These stopped media companies from monetizing adequately the reach they had and from increasing that reach. It was a shock sometimes to know how under-monetized the Indian media industry was (and still is). In 2009, according to one analysis that Media Partners Asia did, TV companies in Brazil which had less than half the TV homes India had had more than twice the margins.

Whether it was pushing for digitization that brought in more pay revenues or splurging on developing half a dozen sports so that they contributed to increasing Star's reach, Shankar went by the book on market development. It is these investments that finally led to the near-trebling of Star's revenues from Rs 4575 crore ($704 million) in the year ending March 2012 to Rs 13,448 crore ($2.06 billion) in March 2018. At some point, in 2015, James Murdoch had said that Star India would hit $500 million (Rs 3250 crore) in EBITDA (earnings before interest, taxes, depreciation and amortization) in fiscal 2018 and $1 billion by fiscal 2020 on the back of these investments. Star's EBITDA in fiscal 2018 was $452 million (Rs 2938 crore).

As usual, we are running ahead of the story.

The making of *Satyamev Jayate*

Satyajit Bhatkal, fifty-four, is as Maharashtrian as they come. He speaks in soft, measured tones, is erudite and musically literate. As a kid studying in Mumbai's Bombay Scottish School, Bhatkal became friends with Aamir Khan. Bhatkal was the more popular student, always among the toppers in the class. Khan, Hindi film producer Tahir Hussain's son, was an average student—the quintessential filmy kid, in Mumbai parlance.

After school, Bhatkal went on to study and practise law for over a decade. He was actively involved in social and political causes and wrote extensively on them. Khan, on the other hand, became a very successful actor, breaking records with his debut film *Qayamat Se Qayamat Tak*. He is now among India's top five stars and is also seen as a thinking man's actor. He chooses his roles carefully, focuses intensely on a single project, sometimes even gets involved financially. For instance, the eclectic story of a bunch of villagers in pre-Independence India who challenge their British rulers to a cricket match fascinated him enough to don the mantle of producer. *Lagaan* (2001) went on to become the third Indian film to be nominated for an Oscar in the Best Foreign Language Film category. His other big films include *3 Idiots* (2009) and *PK* (2014). *3 Idiots* is a funny take on India's education system while *PK* tackles blind superstition that plagues so much of India. Khan's biggest global success is, of course, *Dangal* (2016), which did $310 million at the box office. Of this, $84 million came from India, the rest from outside the country. Almost $200 million was the box office revenue from China, a market totally unfamiliar with Indian films. *Dangal*, the real story of a national-level wrestler who trained his daughters despite the odds, is one of the finest Indian films ever made.

'Seeing Satya's work, I used to always think how is it that I can also be helpful to people. It was something that used to always prick me. As I became more successful in my profession it began to prick me even more,' Khan was quoted as saying in *India Today*.[3] Meanwhile, Bhatkal's experiences as an activist and a lawyer led him to believe he had a story to tell. In his mid-thirties, he quit law to work in film and television.[4] He was part of the core production team of

---

[3] Khan did not give me an interview for this book. This quote is from 'What Led Aamir to Do a Show Like *Satyamev Jayate*' by Faheem Ruhani in *India Today* on 28 August 2014.

[4] Much of this introduction comes from a bio that Bhatkal himself has written for IMDB. I also interviewed him extensively for this book.

Lagaan and also directed, arguably, India's first theatrically released documentary, 'Chale Chalo'. He wrote the very readable bestseller *The Spirit of Lagaan* (2003), which was translated into three Indian languages. Later, he wrote and directed *Bombay Lawyers*, a critically acclaimed mini-series for NDTV in 2007. It dealt with social issues in the format of fictionalized courtroom drama.

In 2010, Khan, now fifty-three, called Bhatkal. Many large broadcasters had tried to tempt him with offers of TV shows; he was the last of the stars not to have done one. Amitabh Bachchan (*KBC*), Shah Rukh Khan (*KBC*, *Kya Aap Panchvi Paas Se Tez Hain*), Salman Khan (*Big Boss*), Akshay Kumar (*Khatron Ke Khiladi*), almost all the big stars had done some TV show or the other. But he didn't want to do plain entertainment or game shows. He wanted to do something that helped give back to society. Could Bhatkal develop a television show on social issues? 'I said yes, I would like to do that,' says Bhatkal. He put together a small team with his usual collaborators: wife Svati Chakravarty and head of research Lancelot Fernandes. 'Aamir had said, place no restrictions on yourself. It could be a game show or a documentary or whatever else. We decided that we couldn't decide on a format sitting there in Mumbai. We needed life and reality to tell us what to do,' says Bhatkal. Soon, journalist Prerana Thakurdesai and film-maker Suresh Bhatia joined the team, and all of them read tonnes of material on the issues they wanted to tackle. By the second half of 2010, they began travelling all over the country.

Svati shot a film on female foeticide, Thakurdesai on health systems, and soon they had six films. Of these, the most important story was Svati's fifty-five-minute film on female foeticide, which moved anyone who saw it. India's preference for sons is reflected in the shameful male–female ratios which can go as low as around 800 women to 1000 men in some states, according to the 2011 Census. In many parts of the country, irrespective of class, Indian families go to any extent to find out the sex of a child and terminate the foetus if it is a female. It is for this reason that India has had a law against sex-determination tests since 1996. The female foeticide film 'taught us that you can take a topic done to death and yet have something compelling to say. The female foeticide story is not about the unborn child but of the mother who has no control over her womb. Seeing them as people who have a life, seeing them in the full tapestry of their lives is very moving. We found it difficult to edit the film,' says Bhatkal.

That is when the team decided that in this show the ordinary people who were impacted by the issue being discussed would take centrestage instead of a star. These were 'people who have done heroic things, whose battle hasn't been brought to newspapers and that is what we were seeing,' recounts Fernandes in a video documenting the making of the show which was born out of this process: *Satyamev Jayate*.

Satyamev Jayate would be about India's most gruesome issues but with a tight focus on who, why and how they could be solved. 'How do we find a way out of it? In India there is no problem that has not already been solved; the only thing is we don't solve it on scale. There will be a village or a district somewhere which has solved, say, the water problem, but that solution doesn't reach the others,' says Bhatkal, who also runs the Paani Foundation now.

Bhatkal and his team edited the six films. These were then screened for Khan and his wife, film-maker Kiran Rao. The format suggested itself from the material. 'All we needed was to thread it together with an anchor who navigates it from the beginning to the end,' says Bhatkal. Khan agreed to be the narrator. 'Aamir is a very conviction driven person. If he is not convinced about something *duniya yahan ki wahan ho jaaye* [the world can shift from here to there] he won't do it,' says Bhatkal. Once Khan thought the show was something he was happy to lend his name to, he brought in Star India. This was in March 2011. 'Uday saw what Aamir saw and his reaction was that he wanted to do the show,' says Bhatkal. That is how *Satyamev Jayate* (or 'truth alone prevails'), a show right after Shankar's heart, was born. Shankar, incidentally, gave it that name.

Khan had two conditions—one, the show should also be aired on the terrestrial public service broadcaster Doordarshan and on rival networks in languages that Star did not broadcast in. Two, it should not be on prime time but on Sunday morning at 11 a.m. He wanted as much reach as possible, wanted families to watch it on a Sunday morning without the distractions of other prime-time shows. This involved complicated manoeuvring. Star had to leverage its own network, that of rivals in other languages it did not have, and get Doordarshan homes in. On Aamir's insistence, it had to put a show with one of India's biggest film stars in the usually moribund Sunday morning slot. Most of it worked.

Bhatkal hired an outside producer but that person wanted to spice up the show. Both Khan and Bhatkal were clear that this show would be direct, honest. To ensure that Aamir Khan Productions took over the onus of producing it. In June 2011, the team shot a pilot on the female foeticide issue. It tested well among different focus groups. Now they needed thirteen topics to fill up a season. These had to be pan-Indian—whether it was child sexual abuse or honour killings or medical negligence. Svati, Shankar, Bhatkal and Khan went into a huddle at Khan's farmhouse in Panchgani, a hill station about 245 km from Mumbai, for a couple of days. Once they were back, work on the show began in earnest. Each episode of the show had 200 to 300 hours of raw footage—interviews or discussions with victims, their friends, families and experts on the subject. For instance, the episode on water had 400 hours of footage. This was then digested by Fernandes and Bhatkal who were at the backend. They had to decide the bits to use. It was gruelling, emotionally exhausting work.

By late 2011, the team was ready to shoot the show. The set was put up in Malad, in northern Mumbai. Funnily enough, the night before the shoot, the set burned down—reminiscent of the disaster that had struck *KBC* on the first day of its shoot when electricity across Mumbai tripped. The team had to move to Yash Raj Studios in Mumbai's Andheri area. 'We were happy because the new set took three months to make and that gave us a breather. Those three months made us better prepared,' says Bhatkal. Prasoon

Joshi, Swanand Kirkire and other lyricists wrote the songs that Ram Sampath composed for each of the thirteen episodes in Season 1.

Satyamev Jayate began airing on 6 May 2012 in eight languages across nine channels, including rival Eenadu TV. The first episode on female foeticide made me cry. In fact, it brought tears to many of the 100 million people who watched it. That and the title song forced us to take a fresh look at things we had become hardened to as a country. Every episode of the show made you cringe, cry or root for change. For instance, it has been years since I saw the episode, but the image of the man who discusses his experience with sexual abuse as a child doesn't go out of my head—or that of his mother whom he confronts for ignoring his pleas for help. The warts of India—and human beings in general—were on display and made for uncomfortable Sunday morning viewing. But the show continued to rise in viewership, hitting over 370 million people at one point. Its unique-to-India blend of celebrity, social issue and great research made for compelling content. There were discussions, protests and debates around it. 'We had started a social conversation on issues like child sexual abuse and female foeticide and it will continue,' said Shankar in a video on the making of the show.

'It was therapy at the national level. It was a big moment for this country. A collective conversation about something that should concern everyone was started,' says Bhatkal. In fact, the whole team of *Satyamev* needed therapy after the show was canned because the research and making of the show was emotionally exhausting and traumatic. Even Khan would end up crying at times. This led to odd situations. 'People thought he was faking it and it became my job to cut his tears out,' says Bhatkal. But to keep it from becoming about him, his time on screen was limited to about a fifth of the show's average run time of sixty-six minutes.

'People would ask us how do people open up to Aamir, aren't they overawed by him,' says Bhatkal. The team was serious about making the victims the stars. The people who were to be part of the show on, say, child sexual abuse or medical negligence would come to Mumbai by air. They were received by the *Satyamev Jayate* team and taken to the set the next morning, just to acclimatize them with how it worked. They would have lunch with Khan on the set. And Khan did not discuss the issues that had brought them there. The shoot actually began on day three, by which time they were familiarized with Mumbai and Khan. 'I got to meet different people from different parts of the country and found what humanity, bravery, being generous were all about. It was not a TV show, it was an experience where we learnt a lot,' said Khan in the video on the making of *Satyamev Jayate*.

The show, which took about a year in the making and cost a reported Rs 4 crore ($0.73 million) an episode, had none of the fun elements of *KBC*—no Bachchan bantering with the participant, no quiz questions. Yet, it touched Indians in a way that even news didn't. It reached a large audience and, according to most people familiar with it, just about broke even.

Satyamev Jayate is important, however, not only because Khan did his first TV show or because it was a form of 'important developmental journalism' on an entertainment channel. It was also a powerful signal that Shankar was firmly and unequivocally in charge, his first mark on the network. He had personally backed the show from the word go. 'The legal team sat through every episode. Many times Uday would override them and say "Jo hoga dekha jaayega" [We will cross that bridge when we come to it],' says Nitin Vaidya, who was executive vice president and general manager, Star Plus. Soon after the first episode on female foeticide, some agencies doing illegal sex-determination tests were exposed. 'Aamir and I went to meet Ashok Gehlot [then chief minister of Rajasthan]. He ordered a judicial inquiry. For any broadcaster, especially a multinational corporation, to do this kind of hard-hitting show was something. There were a few notices, cases filed. But Uday stood firm as a rock,' says Vaidya.

Most of the issues were, in fact, followed up either through government or non-governmental organizations. *Satyamev Jayate* went on to do three seasons, albeit with fewer episodes—five in Season 2 and six in Season 3. Sumantra Dutta, who was with

Star for over twenty years, sums it up best: '*Satyamev Jayate* was Uday's journalistic instinct. It was not a show for an entertainment channel. But it created noise in Delhi, signalled a change and didn't lose money.' Dutta was CEO of the Bangladesh-based media conglomerate Beximco till earlier this year. Currently, he is a business strategy consultant with VFS Global.

The push for digitization, the friendship with Zee

'Uday understood the sociopolitical and cultural dynamics of doing business in India. Anyone else would take time but being a journalist Uday understood the politics,' says Vaidya. He is absolutely right. Shankar was in many ways more Indian than Mukerjea, who had cut his teeth in London and Hong Kong. Unlike Mukerjea, Shankar had no fear of taking on regulators or lobbying for things that could help Star and the industry grow. The biggest of these were pay revenues—stuck in perpetual limbo because of the way the market was structured.

Shankar has, over the years, taken part in every industry forum, been part of committees and bodies within the industry, and continues to do so. He understood that this was the way Star's point of view would be heard. After Shankar joined, Star started identifying the concerns of Indian media companies, enhancing its Indian identity and ensuring that the government or regulator was never suspicious of its agenda. 'One of the things I have worked on is repairing Star's relationship with stakeholders—whether they are cable operators, regulators or rivals like Zee,' said Shankar to me in 2012. He believed that if the issues within the ecosystem—whether revenue leakages or poor programming standards—were not sorted, Star as a leader couldn't grow.

In 2010, Shankar was elected as the chairman of the Indian Broadcasting Federation. The body had become more active fighting for issues like being paid on time by advertisers. Shankar along with fellow broadcasters at Zee, Sony and Viacom18 spent a lot of time and effort lobbying for the digitization of the then Rs 34,000 crore

($7.5 billion) TV broadcasting industry. Pay is the single biggest revenue source for most broadcasters across the world. However, in India, only digitization could unlock this revenue stream, which could bring in a couple of billion dollars into the system. This is why.

Think of cable TV distribution in India as a chain that starts from the signal broadcasters send. Earlier, cable operators picked it up directly and sold these signals to you and me. By the mid-1990s, the number of channels had increased so greatly that it was impossible for small operators with 500 to 1000 homes to keep buying additional dishes and give us more channels. Enter the multisystem operators or MSOs—wholesalers of the signal who invested in huge headends, lots of satellite dishes and control rooms. Think of them as large depots that downlink the 800-plus channels beamed into India and resell it to the 60,000 cable operators all over India. They in turn sell the signals to you and me.

While several metro MSOs like Hathway or InCable had spent money laying fibre optic cable within cities, they had no say in how the signal finally reached the home. Nor could they put in a set-top box—the first step to transparency. A set-top box is like an electric meter but for the television signal. It monitors what a home is viewing and bills it accordingly. In most markets across the world, pay TV began with a set-top box. In India it didn't, thereby creating a basic genetic defect. It meant that cable operators, who controlled a bulk of the cable and satellite homes, could hide their real numbers. And they did. They routinely understated their subscriber base and, therefore, the revenues owed to MSOs (and hence to broadcasters). Broadcasters squeezed a little more from them every year by negotiating higher 'declarations' or more for each home 'declared'.

For example, assume that in 2001 an operator paid ESPN-Star Sports Rs 16 per home for 7 million homes and Star Plus Rs 5 per home for 6 million homes. He might up it to Rs 20 and Rs 8 per home the next year for the same number of homes. This even while everyone knew that these channels probably reached

30 million homes. The game then depended on the channel's pull with viewers—the higher the pull the better the numbers cable operators admitted to and paid for. This also meant cable operators paid less in taxes. Much of the money 'leaked' away—a polite way of saying that it was undeclared income. About three-fourths, maybe more, of local cable systems in India have political affiliations, and cable has, over the years, become a steady source of funding for local elections.

As long as it was a relatively small fifty-to-sixty-channel market with advertising growing in double digits, broadcasters could live with this cheating. But as the number of channels increased and carriage and placement fees came in, everyone started feeling the pressure. Carriage fee is the money cable operators and MSOs take simply to carry a channel, and placement fee is for placing the channel on a better frequency or within the right cluster of channels on a cable system.

By 2005, cable TV pipes in India were beyond their choking point. Most were capable, at best, of carrying 106 satellite channels. Yet, more than 160 were on offer, besides hundreds of local cable channels, like CCC from Hathway or CVO from InCable. The irony was evident. India is a large, heterogeneous market which needed more channels in different languages and genres. The drop in transponder costs globally was fuelling a boom in channels—especially those in Indian languages. But there was no bandwidth to carry them.

Instead of doing something about sorting out this mess, the broadcast regulator, Telecom Regulatory Authority of India (TRAI), however, remained focused on pricing (it still is).

The solution to easing the logjam was simple. The bandwidth needed to carry one analog channel is equal to ten digital ones. To increase bandwidth, reduce distribution costs, improve variety and get a better share of revenues, the cable system in India needed to be digitized and made addressable. But the initiative would not come from cable operators—they did not want to invest Rs 5000 per set-top box and the expensive paraphernalia that went with it and end up showing all that they owed to MSOs. The latter were happy to invest but couldn't considering that they didn't own the last mile.[5]

By 2007, there seemed to be some light at the end of the tunnel. An alternate way of distributing TV signals, DTH was taking off, bringing some succour to broadcasters. A DTH connection is tracked from day one because it is digital, there is a set-top box and every consumer is accounted for. Dish TV, the DTH service from Zee's parent Essel Group, had launched in 2003, and in 2006 came Tata Sky, owned jointly by the Tatas and Star. Sun Direct from the Sun TV family and Reliance DTH (which was later sold) were on the cards. DTH came with the full paraphernalia that pay TV brings—an electronic programming guide and a proper call centre you could gripe at. The first few IPTV or Internet protocol TV experiments were happening—these were sending television signals over the same pipes on which Internet data travelled. Think of it as the early years of streaming video. More than a billion dollars were committed to various technologies that would bring transparency to the distribution of TV signals and, therefore, pay revenues. These were the first signs of a healthy pay ecosystem being built.

This brought some hope to broadcasters who were looking at a slowing ad market post the 2008 Lehman crisis. Even as ad revenue growth slowed down, content and carriage costs had doubled over the four years ending 2011. Pay revenues continued to stagnate at about 10–15 per cent of the top line for most broadcasters. Operating margins for the industry had halved to about 13 per cent over five years. The title of being the world's second-largest cable market had not amounted to much either in returns for investors or profits for media owners.

Meanwhile, DTH had grown to 40 million homes, bringing with it the best proof of what digitization could do. Broadcasters

---

[5] Many of them had enthusiastically invested anything between Rs 100–150 crore ($21–31 million) in set-top boxes and associated tech when conditional access was made mandatory (briefly) in 2002.

were getting a bigger and better share of pay revenues from DTH than from cable, which reached about 80 million homes by then.

There soon came a push for transparency and digitization from broadcasters. They had earlier resisted it thinking they would lose reach and therefore ad revenues.

It was around this time that Star and Zee came together again.

Punit Goenka, forty-three, managing director and CEO, Zee Entertainment Enterprises, was part of the team that led the turnaround of Zee in 2006. He had become the CEO of Zee in 2008 and had done a superb job of turning Zee into the professionally run, rock solid and very profitable company it is. He had bumped into Shankar several times either at IBF meetings or at industry dos. Neither he nor Shankar had any rancour or vestiges of the rivalry and bitterness that dogged Star's earlier relationship with Zee. 'It was a different Star, just as Zee was different. We had no baggage, the agenda was the industry agenda,' says Goenka with a shrug.

At some stage over a drink the two decided that they may compete for ratings but had to put together their heads for digitization. 'Uday [Shankar] and I have been expressing our frustration about the way things are moving in the cable industry and our over-dependence on advertising. We were talking about ways to collaborate, and we figured finally that the only way to make it happen is through distribution,' said Goenka in 2011. That is how they ended up creating Media Pro. 'The old Star or Zee would have never done Media Pro, and it was a reflection of new thinking by two strong new leaders in Uday and Punit,' says Couto about how much things had changed by then.

Star had a joint venture with cable major Den Networks for the distribution of channels: Star-Den. Zee had a tie-up with Turner for distribution called Zee-Turner. Media Pro Enterprises, set up in May 2011, was a 50:50 joint venture between these two firms. It would distribute the seventy-five channels the two firms owned between them and those of other broadcasters. According to estimates from the ratings agency TAM Media Research, the joint venture controlled close to 40 per cent of the total TV viewing in India. This would give Media Pro heft in negotiating for lower carriage fees and better declarations. 'The idea is to strengthen the ecosystem, to ensure that the money that comes in as pay revenues is spread across the value chain and this includes MSOs [multi-system operators],' Goenka had explained to me.

Not everybody was happy. It was labelled as cartelization and forced digitization. It also shook the monopoly of cable operators. Others followed. There was IndiaCast, which Viacom18 did with Sun TV. Media Pro lasted for three years, till a new set of guidelines from TRAI in 2013 meant that aggregation, like what Media Pro was doing, was not allowed. Media Pro was disbanded in 2014. 'It was designed to be a time-bound joint venture; once it served its purpose—gave growth and forced digitization—it was dissolved,' says Goenka.

Media Pro did force the issue of transparency and a better share of pay revenues. The state of the industry, the lobbying and the clearly rising share from DTH finally helped push through an amendment to the Cable Television Networks (Regulation) Act, 1995 late in 2011. This mandated that TV signals could not be sold without addressability—meaning, without a digital set-top box. 'You needed an ordinance because otherwise digitization was not happening. Even if the cable operator is not paying taxes, not declaring revenues, a broadcaster has to give him the signal because of the "must provide" clause.[6] If there was fair competition then digitization would have happened on its own,' said Shankar then.

The industry was happy. A schedule was laid out for the digitizing of all analog cable homes by December 2014. The process eventually lasted till some point in 2017. While there are set-top boxes in a majority of India's 103 million cable TV homes,

---

[6] The rules stated that a broadcaster could not have any exclusive arrangement with distribution companies. He must provide content to all distributors on a non-discriminatory basis.

addressability is a moot point. MSOs or cable companies still have no control over the last mile: your home. When Hathway, a cable firm, says it has 12 million homes, these are homes that it supplies signals to through thousands of small cable operators. Legally, even the cable operator's ownership over your home was (and still is) not clear. In practice, though, he has a death-like grip over it and the revenues. Note that the whole discussion on digitization in this section and the challenges therein is true only for cable homes; the 56 million DTH homes which use Tata Sky or Airtel are digital and addressable to start with.

The push for cable digitization led by the IBF and Shankar increased most broadcasters' share of pay revenues. Currently, Star, Zee and Viacom18 get about a third of their revenues from subscription, though at an industry level the figure remains at 25 per cent. The struggle against price regulation continues, as you will read in the next chapter.

Much of this action on the ground to unlock pay revenues was critical for the next big investments Star was about to make—digital and sports.

The push for sports

Sports had been a focus area for News Corporation ever since Chase Carey took over as deputy chairman, president and COO in 2009. He had been head of DirecTV and was being touted as a successor to Rupert Murdoch within the system. News Corp has bid billions of dollars on football, basketball and other sports in the US. The idea was to take on ESPN's thirty-year-old hegemony in the US. News Corp also believed that sports could be the 'locomotive' to get better revenues from its dominant pay TV platforms such as BSkyB and Sky Italia, among many others. It also de-risks its entertainment and news-led television business. Sports was on Shankar's radar too, especially since 2011. That is because pay TV, the biggest revenue driver for this genre, was in place in India thanks to DTH and mandatory digitization of cable.

In April 2012, Star made its first massive bet to further its sports agenda. It offered the Board of Control for Cricket in India (BCCI) a whopping Rs 3851 crore ($770 million) for media rights to all international cricket played in India and for domestic tournaments such as the Ranji Trophy. These rights covered ninety-six matches being played from 2012 to 2018. The price was 25 per cent over and above the last bid. Around the same time, its parent News Corporation bought out ESPN's share in the pan-Asian joint venture ESPN-Star Sports (now Fox Star Sports Asia) for $220 million (Rs 1056 crore). After the buyout, Star India would own the rights to almost all cricket matches involving India, the English Premier League, Formula 1 and the US Open. The only big tournament it didn't have then was the Indian Premier League (IPL), a nearly-two-month-long cricket hoopla and the most valuable sports property in a cricket-crazy country. (Sony had the IPL rights for ten years ending 2017.) Over the next few months, Star bid for and won the digital rights to the IPL too.

In the financial year ending March 2011, Star India got almost all its Rs 3652 crore ($562 million) in revenues from entertainment. At an estimated Rs 4000 crore ($784 million) in advertising and pay revenues, the sports market was then just under 11 per cent of the television market in India—penetration was growing both online and in linear TV. It made sense to gun for a slice of that pie. That had roughly been the idea when Star had joined hands with ESPN in 1996 but the joint venture never felt like its own. 'Historically, they [Star] felt hamstrung in India and Asia by ESPN,' said Couto when the break-up happened.

Not surprisingly, there was a huge amount of analysis on the ifs and buts of Star's push into sports. There was Sony, which owned the IPL then and was doing a cool Rs 1000–1500 crore ($154–231 million) a year in revenues just on sports programming. Dasgupta had focused on sports soon after Star hit the high times in 2000. Zee had attempted to build its own Indian cricket league or ICL from 2007–09 before giving up. It also bought Ten Sports in 2006 (and sold it to Sony in 2016). There was ESPN. And then there was the market. Almost the entire 2 per cent of the total TV viewing that sports got in 2012 went to cricket and it had been the same for over five years. More than 90 per cent of the Rs 4000 crore ($784 million) that television made on sports went to cricket, specifically to cricket where India was playing. The realization on every ten seconds of advertising time sold has been flat for about three years. Wasn't cricket too mature a category to invest in, asked analysts? Would it pull down Star's operating profits of about 10 per cent from entertainment?

'Margins will come under pressure. But we are not doing this for tactical reasons. We are in this business for the long haul. Just like we have built a robust entertainment franchise, we will build a sports one. If we are such a cricket-crazy country why is only 2 per cent of the viewership coming from cricket? The fundamental problem is increasing the number of people who watch the sport,' Shankar had rationalized. The plan was to amplify big sports events with programming wrapped around it, go beyond English for sports broadcasting, and most important of all: develop other sports.

In November 2013, with the launch of six sports channels, Star announced that it would be spending a massive Rs 20,000 crore ($3.6 billion) on sports programming. Of this, 30–40 per cent— or roughly twice the size of the entire sports broadcast industry— would go to non-cricket sports.

In 2000, Star had changed the rules of entertainment with its massive bet on *KBC*. It would now do the same with sports.

11

The Star That Shankar Made

Kabaddi, IPL, Hotstar and a skirmish with regulators

'Look at my body, do you think I can play kabaddi?' asks Shah Rukh Khan. One of India's biggest superstars was facing a barrage of reporters and photographers gathered at the National Sports Club of India (NSCI) grounds in Mumbai. The whole club looked and felt like a carnival venue. It was Saturday, 26 July 2014, and the opening match of the newly established Pro Kabaddi League was about to begin. Somebody had asked Khan if he intended to play. Kabaddi is a rough game played between two teams, each comprising seven well-built young men, and Khan is slight and middle-aged. He had played hockey in college, but kabaddi was clearly not his sport.

Khan was part of the who's who of corporate India, films and sports who walked into NSCI that evening much to the delight of the reporters and the audience. Actor Abhishek Bachchan, the owner of Jaipur Pink Panthers, came in with wife and former Ms World Aishwarya Rai and dad and superstar Amitabh Bachchan. Jaipur Pink Panthers was competing against media baron Ronnie Screwvala's U Mumba that night (U Mumba won). Young heart-throb Ranbir Kapoor, Aamir Khan and cricketer Sachin Tendulkar were amongst those present. For a league that nobody wanted the broadcast rights for and for which team franchises were sold by calling in favours from friends, this was unexpectedly great going. 'Nobody believed that kabaddi would have value. But there was no looking back from the opening night,' recalls Anand Mahindra, chairman, Mahindra Group, and co-founder of the Pro Kabaddi League.

Over five weeks, as eight teams battled one another, more than 128 million people tuned in to various Star channels to watch the first season of the league. By 2016, just two years later, kabaddi had become the second-most-watched sport after cricket, reaching 232 million people against 361 million for the IPL, the biggest sporting event in India. By 2018 this comparison stood at 297 million for the Pro Kabaddi League versus 448 million viewers for cricket's IPL. In many Indian states—Andhra Pradesh, Telangana, Maharashtra and Karnataka—kabaddi beats cricket on viewership according to data from the audience measurement body, Broadcast Audience Research Council (BARC). The number of teams is up from eight to twelve, the games are bigger, and the season is longer at thirteen weeks instead of the original five.

'From where it was five years ago to where it is today, it is simply phenomenal,' says Nitin Kukreja, CEO, iQuest Enterprises, which owns the Tamil Thalaivas. Kabaddi has been the most extraordinary success on television and on the ground in a country obsessed with cricket. It is no longer a novelty to see city kids playing this rustic game in local parks. 'At dinners I have had moms walk up and say, "When will kabaddi get over?" Kids are watching it during prime time [8–10 p.m.] when the women want to watch TV,' laughs Srini Sreeramaneni, managing director, Core Green Group, and a part of Veera Sports, which owns Telugu Titans.

The story of kabaddi is also the story of how far and how seriously Shankar has taken the whole 'develop new markets, expand the market' idea that drives his thinking for Star. It is now, along with Star's regional business, its video app Hotstar and the rights to IPL, one of the big valuation drivers for the firm. In 2015 Shankar pointed out to me that sports and regional markets were the two big growth planks he had pitched for when he became CEO of Star in 2007. While the Asianet acquisition happened in 2008, other investments were held back as the global economy slowed down in the wake of the Lehman crisis and the India sentiment weakened. By 2012–13, when things settled down a bit, he went for the jugular.

Some senior managers from Star reckon that kabaddi, IPL and Hotstar happened precisely because Star needed to drive up valuation since the Murdochs had begun to think of selling 21st Century Fox. Possibly. The story is fascinating for three reasons. One, Shankar's chutzpah in betting big money on one business after another. Two, New York's unreserved backing for him. Three, the plan has largely worked. Like kabaddi, none of the new businesses are profitable as yet, and they won't be for some time. Still, they have added almost three times as much heft to Star's revenue—from Rs 4575 crore ($704 million) in March 2012 the figure stood at a gargantuan Rs 13,448 crore ($2.06 billion) in March 2018. Star is a standard part of any analyst's conversation with 21st Century Fox and, lately, Disney.

Most Indians grow up playing, watching or knowing kabaddi. It is part of our DNA, like antakshari (see Chapter 3, 'Murugan Shoots for Murdoch'), but nobody ever gave it much thought or television time. Bringing it back to our consciousness and giving it the platform it deserves counts amongst Star's biggest achievements. 'If Star had not taken a bet on it, I doubt if kabaddi would have taken off. Seventy per cent of the credit goes to Star because of the amount of push and advertising they have put behind it,' believes Sreeramaneni of Telugu Titans.

The remaining—and possibly even more valuable—30 per cent would go to Anand Mahindra and Charu Sharma.

Kabaddi, kabaddi, kabaddi

Kabaddi is a combative sport played between two teams, each with seven players. It is played for a period of forty minutes with a five-minute break.[1] The idea is to score points by raiding the opponent's court and touching as many defence players as possible—without getting caught—in a single breath. The one-breath rule has been scrapped in the Pro Kabaddi League. One player saying 'kabaddi, kabaddi, kabaddi' charges into the rival's court and tries to touch the opponents closest to him within thirty seconds. The opposing team, meanwhile, tries to catch the raider. Its origin, says the Amateur Kabaddi Federation of India website, dates backs to prehistoric times. This cross between wrestling and rugby is hugely popular in rural India and there are thousands of kabaddi clubs and teams. It has brought medals for India internationally, but much like other sports, never captured popular attention the way cricket did. Cricket dominates the sports economy, media time and even the state's attention. No other sport in India is as rich or as pampered, or has a self-sustaining ecosystem like cricket. Stadiums, sponsors, players, facilities, it has everything that kabaddi—usually played in the mud—never did.

In 2006, Mahindra's brother-in-law and well-known sports anchor Charu Sharma brought the game to his attention. Sharma had just returned from an assignment at the 15th Asian Games in Doha, Qatar, and had been struck by the enormous interest kabaddi had generated amongst non-Indian spectators. For the first time in the history of the Asian Games a separate indoor stadium had been built for kabaddi. There were rubberized mats, giant screens and a running score. Much of this helped showcase the game to the Europeans and Australians who were closely involved in organizing the Games in the small, rich desert nation. Many spectators from these and other nations who were watching the game for the first time were impressed with the simple rules and the sheer thrill of

---

[1]   Some of these basic rules of the game are from the Amateur Kabaddi Federation of India website.

action. They wanted to introduce the sport in their countries. Till then, other than India, only a few countries including Iran and Korea played kabaddi at an international level.

'I told Anand [Mahindra] that this is a fabulous game for you to promote,' says Sharma. It remained what it was, just a conversation. When IPL took off in 2008, Mahindra received offers to be a part of it as well as the incipient Indian Soccer League. He was, however, inclined to look for other, less championed sports and use the league format to dramatically improve the fortunes of the sport.

The $14.5 billion (Rs 93,896 crore) Mahindra Group has interests across automobiles, software and financial services. The conglomerate is first and foremost about tractors and also has a strong presence in the Indian automobile market. It is the world's largest manufacturer of tractors. Farm equipment, of which tractors is a huge part, forms close to 17 per cent of its top line. Mahindra had wanted to associate with a sport like kabaddi because of its rural fit. He attempted through 2011 to start a kabaddi league within Mahindra's farm equipment division. But 'they didn't "get it". They came back to me with a proposal to sponsor the national championship,' says Mahindra ruefully.

At some point in 2011, Mahindra and Heidi Ueberroth, then president of the American National Basketball Association (NBA) International were waiting for Lalit Modi at the Four Seasons in Mumbai. The Mahindra Group had promoted a community basketball league in association with the NBA. Modi had been the commissioner of the IPL, the most successful sports league in India. Talk turned to the promotion of sports other than cricket and Mahindra, who had kabaddi on his mind, asked Ueberroth if she had seen it. 'She had and believed it to be ideally suited for television, given the small arena, and the aggressive, fast-paced action it showcased—plus the fact that it was over in forty-forty-five minutes,' says Mahindra.

The chat with Ueberroth excited him. He reached out to Sharma and proposed that they jointly create a kabaddi league. 'And I said why not? I would do the running around and Anand [Mahindra] would be the owner [and put in money in his personal capacity],' says Sharma, a polite, precise sort of person.

That is how Mashal Sports—owned by Sharma, Mahindra, corporate lawyer Rajiv Luthra and adman Piyush Pandey— approached the Amateur Kabaddi Federation of India.[2] Mashal got the rights to hold the league for ten years.[3] Getting people to bid for team franchises proved to be a tough task. Mahindra called his friends, many of them amongst the super rich in India, such as banker Uday Kotak and retailer Kishore Biyani. Both became team owners. Kotak and Biyani apart, Sharma and Mahindra were invariably greeted with barely concealed disbelief whenever they made their pitch to prospective team owners.

'To be fair, one could hardly have expected anyone to jump at an "opportunity" to own a team in what was perceived to be an anachronistic, crude, rural sport. For urban dwellers this was a picnic sport. Most of the franchisees came in as an act of faith and also because that act didn't require anywhere near as much investment as for an IPL team,' laughs Mahindra. The Pro Kabaddi League teams in Season 1 sold for as little as Rs 1 crore as against the tens of crores of rupees for an IPL team, according to one estimate. When a franchisee backed out, Mahindra called Rajesh Shah (co-chairman and managing director, Mukand Steel) and asked him to bid for Patna Pirates. 'It won the league title three times in a row,' says a delighted Mahindra. 'I have a deep and strong interest in sports. I knew nothing about kabaddi, but the people involved were good so I invested,' says Shah.

The next task was getting a television producer on board. Sharma had spent almost his entire professional life on television so he knew most of the people concerned. He met almost all the big broadcasters. 'They were very kind, they met me but were

---

[2]   Mashal was formed in 1994. From 2011 it became only about the Pro Kabaddi League.

[3]   'In 2013 the agreement was amended to provide for a review and then an extension for an additional five years on similar terms,' says Anand Mahindra.

perplexed. Many put me on to the commercial team, which would give unworkable contracts. We had started in 2011 but we were well into 2012 without making any headway,' remembers Sharma.

Around then Star India had started placing its big bets on sports. It had bought the rights to six years of India cricket from the BCCI. Mashal Sports approached Star. First Luthra met COO Sanjay Gupta. Then Sharma had a meeting with him. 'I tried to convince him that it was a good game for TV. I had a video which showed the journey of kabaddi, how it was played at the Asian Games on rubberized mats. The showcasing was of an Indian sport made international. At the end of it he was neutral but positive. He put me on to the commercial department. The terms were not so good, but they were better than those offered by most other broadcasters,' says Sharma. Star paid a paltry sum, say insiders. But Sharma and Mahindra were happy to have a big broadcaster on board.

On a work trip to New York in October 2013 Mahindra got a call from Shankar, who asked if they could meet. The two met for lunch at the Harvard Club. 'He said that he'd met the Murdochs and told them that kabaddi had the potential to be second only to cricket in terms of followers and viewership. However, a cautious and incremental approach to building the sport would simply not work. The task, in his mind, was to explode onto the sporting scene and ensure that right from the first season, kabaddi is seen as a "cool" sport, especially by urban dwellers,' remembers Mahindra. Shankar apparently recognized that the money Star had agreed to pay for the broadcast rights did not leave much scope for Mashal to make any big investments in stadiums, marketing or any of the things needed to develop the game.

BCCI, the league owner of the IPL for instance, invests in popularizing the league. It could do that by taking the game to more venues, the ways in which rights (digital, broadcast, global or others) are broken up and put up for bidding. Sony TV, which held the broadcast rights to the IPL till 2017, invested huge amounts of money and airtime in promoting the game as well. Its promos, hoardings and on-air ads promoting the IPL have won creative awards at various forums. The idea is to get as many people as possible to watch the game, live, on TV and online. A bigger audience means more in ticket money, sponsorship and advertising. It is good for everyone—the players, the teams, the league and the broadcaster. Given that kabaddi was an unknown quantity, no broadcaster was willing to make the investment and the league (which Mashal owned) didn't have that kind of money.

'He [Shankar] offered that Star would, on its own, invest a significant amount for resources, both in terms of channel time as well as production costs, provided they could take an equity stake in the league, thus sharing in the upside,' says Mahindra. That way Star could invest in production, marketing and building up the game.

Mahindra thought the offer through. 'I decided that if Shankar was going to invest the large sums of money he was hinting at, and in order to ensure seamless management of this new and experimental league, it would be best if I offered Star a majority stake. So I told him, "If you are going to buy then take a controlling stake; we can't have two people running the ship",' says Mahindra. Shankar was taken aback, pleasantly so. They shook hands over lunch.

By November that year Star had announced that it would be spending Rs 20,000 crore ($3.6 billion) on sports programming, about 30 to 40 per cent of which was to go to non-cricket sports. Kabaddi was a big part of it.

'To Star's credit, they jumped right in and began pumping up their involvement and their investments in production capability even before the written agreement had been put down,' says Mahindra.

Sharma soon held a press conference in Mumbai to announce the league and show a demo match. This was followed by more meetings in Mumbai in April 2014. Star agreed to pick up a 74 per cent stake in Mashal Sports and did so in March 2015, after the first season. 'I give Uday a lot of credit; he put in a lot of money. His backing, the way he got cameramen from rugby and built up this game—I didn't have great ambitions when we started,' says Mahindra. Sreeramaneni agrees. He points out that many leagues came in after the Pro Kabaddi League—for badminton, soccer and hockey—but none worked as well. 'Uday took that call because at heart he is a journalist and a content guy,' says he.

The same magic hasn't worked with football or other sports so far. 'All the local league development we are doing [kabaddi, football, hockey] . . . we knew it would take time. But in the long run the economy of cricket will be challenged. And we are building assets for such a time in the future. Everybody is very hung up on the money we are spending on sports [Rs 20,000 crore]. But that is being spent over eight years,' said Shankar to me at the time.

Murdoch was thrilled enough with the India story to say this in the 2014 annual report: 'In India, our operations are stronger than ever, and, with a weekly reach of more than 650 million viewers, Star India remains that nation's largest and most influential entertainment company. The return of the popular and poignant *Satyamev Jayate* was watched by more than 300 million people, and more than 50 million viewers participated online in support of the show's "vote of change" initiatives. Star Sports has also made major sports investments in the past twelve months, launching six networks which deliver the best in cricket, soccer and more to viewers throughout India. Star Sports' commitment to fostering a multi-sports culture is widely known, as evidenced by its investment in the Pro Kabaddi League, a game which was nearly forgotten but with Star's support has been transformed into a modern sporting experience that quickly attracted large and passionate audiences.'

For the Murdochs and Fox, kabaddi is exactly the sort of long-term, category-building, market-shifting initiative they get excited about. 'We've essentially invested all of our profits for the last two years in the entertainment business into building that sports business. And it's been driven by domestic and national teams, India cricket matches. So, there [is] cricket and more recently sports like kabaddi which is a thousand, multi-thousand-year-old sport in India that we've really, in the last two years, professionalized, glamorized, put it on TV, made it a bigger thing. It's been very, very successful, and we have a partner in that. But we control the league there as well, so it's actually really an upstream business for us,' said James at a Bernstein Strategic Decision conference call in 2016.

James was not exaggerating. Ownership of the league is critical to Star's ability to make money on the Pro Kabaddi League. So far the numbers of both the revenues and investment in kabaddi remain small relative to Star's size and staying power. The cumulative investment in the Pro Kabaddi League is estimated to be upwards of $100 million (Rs 700 crore). On an average Star is investing roughly Rs 180 crore to Rs 200 crore ($28 million to $31 million) a year in kabaddi. The break-even is likely by 2021–22, say analysts. That is, if Star continues to hold the media rights.

The Pro Kabaddi League's success has been attributed to the fact that unlike in other sports, Star has end-to-end control. It is media rights owner, broadcaster and league owner. This is unusual in the sporting world—leagues usually put up broadcast rights for bidding and make money from it, as BCCI does with the rights to the IPL.

But the league's viewership in Season 6 in 2018 fell by 31 per cent compared to Season 5 in 2017. It is still huge, second only to the IPL, but the fall in viewership has created rumblings about the conflict of interest that Star faces as a league owner which also owns broadcast rights. Many of the early franchisees who have broken even think media rights, which are up for bidding in 2019 for the 2020 edition, should go to the highest bidder. But going by what Mahindra says, the rights will be up for review and extension by five years on the same terms once the first term ends.[4] When Star took up PKL in 2013 nobody was interested, and it got the rights cheap. The money and effort it spent in building the game are finally paying off and several broadcasters and video-streaming firms are now interested in the league. If it cannot retain the rights, what happens to break-even is a big question. Can it make up as plain

---

[4] Charu Sharma did not respond to my emails and messages to understand how long Mashal has the rights for. Most of Star India did not speak to me for this book.

league owner what it can't as the prime mover and media rights owner? These are the questions that Disney will deal with by and by.

Let us go back to 2015 for now.

The Hotstar story

In 2000 Murdoch had been intrigued enough to spend over $100 million on a handful of Internet start-ups in India. None of them worked out and the investments were written off. Murdoch had been an Internet sceptic for years. In 2009 he called Google a 'content kleptomaniac' and 'parasite' and News Corp blocked it from indexing content from *The Times* and *Sunday Times*. (Two years later, it was back on Google.) It was not that he was an old-media baron who couldn't see the future. He had proved over the years that his view of the way ahead was clearer than that of almost all other media barons—remember he invested in satellite TV technology in the 1980s. It was just that the Internet's time hadn't yet come. It simply didn't have the scale and the revenues that could sustain the investment that mainstream media companies make in content. Google made revenues by throwing up content created by mainstream media, but without sharing them. It still does.

After Indya.com (a pet project of James), Star took another shot at digital with Star Player, a video service on its website, in 2009. It offered full episodes, divided into short-duration videos, of shows from its twenty channels. But this too petered out.

However, a series of events began to indicate that the nature of the game was changing. Every major media firm in India was looking seriously at the Internet for four reasons.

One, in the US, Netflix had started chipping away at pay TV subscribers. Netflix, a video rental service set up in 1997, had morphed into a streaming service by 2007. It started picking up subscribers steadily. However, it shot onto the media scene with its first original show—*House of Cards*—in 2013. Coming at $8–12 a month against the $40–80 that American households usually paid for cable, Netflix seriously disrupted the pay TV market as consumers started cutting the TV cord. YouTube, a free service, was already huge and there were several other video apps coming up. It was clear that this was the way the rest of the world would go. Film studios and broadcasters were worried—they did not want to be caught trying to salvage their businesses à la print publishers. Most had their digital plays, either individually (like HBO) or through Hulu, a streaming service that was launched in 2007. Hulu's investors/partners included media firms such as Walt Disney, 21st Century Fox, AT&T and Comcast.

Two, the India numbers were staggering. In 2015, there were over 970 million mobile phone connections. Some people had more than one connection, so there was duplication. The figure for Indians with a decent broadband connection was closer to 300 million. Of these, about 100 million people were watching video regularly, largely on handheld devices. Though the revenues that online video got remained low at Rs 1500 crore ($242 million), they were already rising in double digits. The inflection point seemed around the corner.

Three, Star had been amongst the top ten channels from India on YouTube for several years by then. At 70 million unique users in India in 2015, YouTube was and remains the biggest video platform and, more importantly, the context in which video has been consumed online. 'We realized that a large number of our viewers were consuming content away from TV screens. We were putting small amounts of our library content on YouTube and getting huge traction. And then there were all kinds of sites where content was being put up and people were watching,' said Shankar at the Asia-Pacific Video Operators Summit in Bali in April 2015. But being on YouTube was not the best option. 'We were not happy because our content was just sitting cheek by jowl with some jumping cat somewhere and some badly made video and here is the drama that your team has spent months and years developing . . . It's like putting a high-quality painting next to someone's dumb stuff,' said Shankar.

Four, the focus on sports meant that digital had to follow. Sports, like news, is globally a huge driver of video consumption online.

And here was Star sitting on loads of cricket content, including the digital rights to the IPL, all of kabaddi and India cricket amongst a host of other things. Star decided that it was time to go online with all guns blazing.

'When we did Indya.com or Star Player we had limited expectations. The scale and depth of the current attempt is significant. Eighteen months ago when we started thinking and planning this [Hotstar], we decided to go only with the mobile,' said Sanjay Gupta, COO (then), in an interview around the launch of Hotstar in 2015. The challenge in India had never been content—it has a robust content ecosystem. It was always technology and bandwidth—whether in TV or on digital. As a broadcaster Star recognized that. To deal with the disparity in bandwidth, operating systems and handsets, there were versions of programming that could work across 7000 variations of operating systems and screen sizes. Star invested in the tech behind its video app. On the content side, there was a tweaking of format. For example, most American shows would have thirteen episodes a season with a total of about 100 hours over eight years. Indian shows go up to 1000 hours in seven years. This makes discovering a show or an episode a nightmare. This was tackled by organizing drama episodes in chapters of fifteen to twenty episodes around a theme.

Hotstar launched in February 2015 on the back of a massive publicity campaign. By May 2015 it was at 50 million unique users. It was, claims Star, the fastest adoption for any digital service in the world. 'Outside of China, for the first time, there is a player who has managed to stand up to Netflix and YouTube. Where has Netflix ever competed with a player which is a broadcaster with huge entertainment content, layered with sports and deep local production capabilities?' asked Shankar in the wake of Hotstar's success. To which added Gupta, 'Our network share of viewership in India is meaningful [about 22 per cent all-India across all of Star's channels then]. It is not 5 or 8 per cent. Therefore, Hotstar becomes a meaningful destination [against being an aggregator].'

The timing of Hotstar's launch was perfect—just before the big bandwidth boom that came with the launch of Jio in 2016. Hotstar rode that boom. The most ambitious telecom launch seen anywhere, from India's largest private sector company, Mukesh Ambani's Reliance Industries, Jio sent data prices crashing from Rs 269 per GB in 2014 to Rs 19 per GB by mid-2018. And consumption doubled from 0.86 GB to 1.6 GB per subscriber per month within a year (from 2016 to 2017). By 2018 this had moved up to a gargantuan 8.4 GB per subscriber per month. Think of it this way—a full-length feature film needs just under 1 GB of data. In 2018, therefore, Indians were consuming content that is the equivalent of eight feature films every month.

By 2017 the Indian over-the-top market, or OTT as streaming apps are called, had turned into a madhouse. Voot from Viacom18, SonyLIV, Viu from PCCW and HOOQ from SingTel were amongst the thirty-five video apps on offer. These belonged to large tech, media or telecom firms. Most, even the ones from smaller players such as ALTBalaji from Balaji Telefilms, had raised between Rs 100 crore to Rs 500 crore ($16 million to $78 million) to cash in on the potential that India, by then the world's fastest growing video market, showed. Hotstar has so far managed to stay ahead. In April 2019 Hotstar was at 128 million unique users, second only to YouTube's 274 million, going by comScore data. Hotstar claims it is at 300 million monthly active users. There is usually a 25–40 per cent difference between the numbers from Google Analytics that most firms share and the ones comScore comes up with. For the sake of consistency, I go with comScore numbers. Whichever way you look at it, Hotstar remains amongst the top three apps along with YouTube and Times Group's MX Player (106 million unique users) in a market with 550 million broadband users.[5]

The three things that drive traffic on Hotstar are catch-up TV, sports and films. A bulk of the people coming on to Hotstar regularly watch *Nimki Mukhiya* or *Yeh Rishta Kya Kehlata Hai*, or

---

[5] Telecom Regulatory Authority of India data for February 2019.

other shows from Star. Another huge wave comes in during the IPL or Pro Kabaddi League seasons, whichever big event is going on. This recedes after the season. Then there is a small slice of audiences for the latest English shows, say *Game of Thrones* or *Koffee with Karan*. Except for sports then, Hotstar mimics the experience of all the other streaming apps from broadcasters such as Voot and Zee5, where catch-up TV is the big driver. But sports is probably the reason why its numbers are far higher than those of the other apps—though there is no break-up of the traffic by type of content.

On revenues, though, Hotstar remains small—not surprising given that online video got just about Rs 6340 crore ($0.9 billion) in advertising and pay revenues in 2018, going by EY data. The estimate was that Star would spend over Rs 1200 crore ($190 million) in the first five years. Gupta had predicted a break-even in five years. Going by data from the Registrar of Companies, Novi Digital, the firm under which Hotstar operates, had by the financial year ending 2017 spent close to Rs 1600 crore ($235 million) on the app. In the same year it had made revenues of Rs 320 crore ($47 million) and losses of Rs 489 crore ($72 million). Media Partners Asia estimates that Hotstar will generate $350 million (Rs 2275 crore) in overall revenues in 2019—thanks to IPL. If it does, then it will be very close to YouTube on revenues.[6]

That brings us to why, across the world, it is tough to make money online. To begin with, the cost per mille/thousand, or CPM, was low at Rs 100–300 viewers compared to Rs 150–1000 on TV. It has increased phenomenally since then to average about four to five times better rates than TV. But even so the benefit of these improved terms goes to only two players—YouTube and Facebook—since they set the rules of the game. Their algorithms determine what will work or won't. Google commands almost a third of the $266 billion in global online ad revenues and over

---

[6] The rupee–dollar conversion of recent figures in this section has been done at Rs 65 to the dollar since Media Partners Asia has used that rate. This is for consistency of comparison.

92 per cent of all searches. That is true for India as well where Google gets a bulk of the Rs 15,400 crore ($2.3 billion) in online ad revenues. Just YouTube India is estimated at Rs 2000 crore ($308 million) in revenues in fiscal 2018. That makes it a largish broadcaster by Indian standards.

Luckily, pay is emerging as a solution—almost every second app now has a pay element. In 2018, of its 128 million users, ErosNow had 13 million subscribers paying anywhere between Rs 50 to Rs 100 a month. Netflix, which is priced at Rs 500 to Rs 800 a month, is estimated to reach close to 1 million subscribers in India. Overall, consumers paid Rs 1340 crore (about $206 million) as subscription for online video in 2018, says EY. The traction on pay, not just in video but in publishing and other categories, has been heartening in India.

Note that the battle in India is different from that in developed markets where cord-cutting is hitting the TV business. India's Rs 74,000 crore ($10.7 billion) TV industry is still in growth mode. In 2018, television viewership rose by 13 per cent over 2017, and total viewers rose to 836 million. This is up from 790 million in 2016 going by data from BARC. The 550 million Indians with broadband connections spend about fifty minutes a day watching online video. This is far below the average three hours and forty-five minutes (and growing) spent on TV. In fact, 2018, the year that OTT finally took off, was a bumper year for Indian films. This is because online adds an extra screen or two to every home in what is largely a single-TV-home market. Therefore, its growth has so far been supplementary and not cannibalistic.

For now then, Hotstar is doing what Star has always done in this market, expanding the pie in its bid to increase its share.

But are there limits to how much you can expand a market? Was Star pushing those limits?

Taking TRAI to court

Deepak Jacob, Star's legal head, is sharp and aggressive. His background in technology and telecom put him in a great position to join a media firm. As soon as he came to Star in 2008 he was pushed into the deep end with the Asianet deal, which ran in parallel with the legal falling out with Balaji. Then came new agreements with producers, the BCCI cricket rights deal and the whole legal framework around the Pro Kabaddi League. Jacob has been on a roller coaster ever since he came to Star. He has in the process become, along with Sanjay Gupta, a key part of Shankar's team. Unlike Mukerjea who was chary of regulators, Jacob and Shankar have been vocal about the issues around the pay ecosystem. They spend time and effort in making the regulator aware of the issues through industry forums and bodies. In spite of Murdoch's reputation as a ruthlessly ambitious man with no respect for rules, in India his company has largely steered clear of getting into skirmishes with regulators.

That changed in 2016.

TRAI became India's broadcast regulator early in 2004 in the wake of attempts to bring in addressability. One of the first things it did was freeze channel prices, allowing only for occasional inflationary adjustments. While TRAI has done a huge amount of work in cleaning up the complicated relationships amongst multisystem operators, cable operators and broadcasters, its 'telecom' mindset has meant a fixation on price control rather than facilitating growth. In the fifteen years that it has been around, it has still not addressed the basic issue of last-mile ownership of cable homes (see Chapter 10, 'Star Sports a New Look'). In terms of the contribution of pay revenues, therefore, things remain exactly the way they were fifteen years ago.

Of India's 197 million TV homes, about 103 million are on cable.[7] Of the rest, over 35 million are on Doordarshan's free DTH service, DD Freedish. Just over 56 million are pay DTH homes. In 2018, India's Rs 74,000 crore ($10.7 billion) TV industry made roughly Rs 43,500 crore ($6.3 billion) from pay revenues. Of this,

---

[7] 'A Billion Screens of Opportunity, India's Media & Entertainment Sector', a report done by EY for FICCI-Frames 2019, the flagship industry event. Almost all the industry numbers from 2017 onwards are based on EY's reports.

only Rs 11,000 crore ($1.6 billion) or one-fourth went back to broadcasters according to EY. Much of this Rs 11,000 crore comes from pay DTH, a smaller part of the TV universe compared to cable. That is because DTH has been digital and addressable from the word go.

In October 2016 TRAI issued a consultation paper on a draft tariff order. It divided broadcast content into devotional, general entertainment, kids et al. It also prescribed a maximum price for each genre with a cap of Rs 19. It placed a 15 per cent cap on discounts offered on bundles. In December 2016 Star India and its Vijay TV filed a petition against the Department of Industrial Policy and Promotion, Department of Telecommunications, Ministry of Information and Broadcasting and TRAI in the Madras High Court. It questioned TRAI's authority to regulate pricing since it was anointed broadcast regulator to regulate 'carriage' in 2004. Content was beyond its authority—a point several experts had been making for years.

Star's petition stated that TRAI's tariff orders and regulations for 'broadcasting services' encroached on the statutory rights that broadcasters enjoy under the Copyright Act of 1957. These laws are based on international treaties to which India is a signatory. Implementing the order would have the effect of regulating content creation, generation, exploitation and licensing, which fall under the Copyright Act. Late in December 2016 the Madras High Court restrained TRAI from notifying and thereby implementing the tariff order.[8] In response to an appeal from TRAI in March 2017 the Supreme Court allowed TRAI to notify its tariff order and asked the Madras High Court to wrap up the case in two months.[9]

---

[8]   *Star India and Vijay TV v. Department of Industrial Policy and Promotion, Department of Telecommunications, Ministry of Information and Broadcasting and Telecom Regulatory Authority of India*, in the High Court of Madras, 23 December 2016.

[9]   *Financial Express*, 'TRAI gets Supreme Court Nod to Notify Tariff Order for TV Channels', 4 March 2017.

When TRAI took over in 2004 there were several arguments for price regulation. The biggest was the mess in cable, practically the only technology offering TV signals at the time. Today, Indian television is competitive across the value chain—in content production (thousands of production houses), distribution (DTH, cable, IPTV, Internet, mobile) and broadcasting (more than 800 channels). Where then is the need for price regulation?

It seemed like a solid case and Star went hammer and tongs to make its point. Funnily enough, the broadcasting industry, while tacitly supporting the litigation, remained silent publicly. Nobody wanted to mess with the regulator. However, after several twists and turns, when the case finally landed in the Supreme Court, it ruled in TRAI's favour in October 2018.[10] But it took away some of the teeth from the order by knocking out the 15 per cent cap on discounts offered on bundles. The tariff order, in all its contradictory complexities, is being implemented, albeit with some changes.

The point of this story is not so much the actual impact of the tariff order. It is about Star and Shankar's confidence in the company being so Indian that it could pick a fight with the regulator, which no Indian company had dared to. Maybe it is his grounding as a political reporter in the Hindi heartland. Maybe it is simply his confidence in what Star has achieved.

At what point could it become overconfidence is a question that many had begun asking. That is a question that will be answered only in 2022 when we have a report card on what the IPL did for Star India.

The bet on the IPL

The IPL was formed in 2007 by the BCCI in reaction to Subhash's Chandra's attempts to set up the Indian Cricket League or ICL. Kunal

---

[10]   In the Supreme Court of India, Civil Appellate Jurisdiction, *Star India v. Department of Industrial Policy and Promotion & Others*. Civil appeal nos. 7326-7327, 30 October 2018.

Dasgupta, the former CEO of Sony, had used sports very effectively to counter Star's prime-time hegemony over entertainment. He saw the potential in the IPL and reportedly bid a (then) gargantuan $1 billion or Rs 4900 crore for the rights to broadcast the IPL for ten years. The twenty-over, carnival-like version of cricket has gone on to become the biggest sporting event in India. By 2017 it had a viewership of 411 million and had, over a decade, brought in close to $2.5 billion in revenues for Sony.

But Sony's ten years were up and there was now a huge amount of interest in the IPL from not just broadcasters but telecom players such as Jio or social media giants such as Facebook. In September 2017 Star India bid for and won the global and India rights across TV and digital to the IPL. Shankar was delighted. Winning the IPL completed the sports portfolio he'd been building up. 'It is no longer about the traditional media firms trying to outbid each other. There are telecom companies, technology firms and social media firms. So I am happy that a media player was able to hold the fort. And also because we got it for a sensible price that is only marginally higher than the other bids,' said Shankar. If the highest bids in each category were combined then Star's composite bid price of Rs 16,348 crore ($2.5 billion) for all rights for five years was just about Rs 527 crore ($81 million) or over 3 per cent more than the others separately. Star made lower bids for individual rights—say digital or TV—but made the only composite bid. Which means it had to estimate, as accurately as possible, how much Facebook, Jio, Sony or others would pay for only digital or TV rights. It made the bidding riskier—it was all or nothing in typical Murdoch style.

'We strongly believe and we would not have bid for the IPL at that price without being absolutely confident that we can still hit our $1 billion EBITDA target by calendar 2020,' said a triumphant Lachlan Murdoch, executive chairman, 21st Century Fox, at a Goldman Sachs Communacopia Conference in the same month. 'IPL was a fantastic win. We needed a strong cricket portfolio to drive sports reach. And to make sports channels available to all users on our baseline,' says a happy Jacob.

There are, however, big questions marks regarding Star's ability to make money on the IPL for two reasons.

One, its Hindi general entertainment business, which is financing much of the splurging on sports, has been challenged for a while now. Hindi general entertainment channels or GECs lost just over a fifth of their viewership in the three years ending 2018. From 28 per cent in 2015 the share of Hindi GECs in total TV viewing fell to 22 per cent in 2018, going by BARC data. This even while overall TV viewing increased by 37 per cent from 22.4 billion impressions[11] in 2016 to 30.7 billion in 2018.

The ostensible reason was that the measurement universe had changed. From a panel of 20,000 homes that covered about 90,000 people, BARC now has 40,000 homes covering over 1,80,000 people and going up. One-third of the sample is now rural with south India having a significant share, though BARC refuses to reveal how much. As a result, the share of non-Hindi GECs has been going up; not just because more people are watching but because more of those watching are getting captured in the sample. But if that was the case why was Star Plus hit worse than Sony (a more urban channel) and Zee TV? Both of them actually did very well. Currently, Star and Zee are almost neck and neck on overall audience share, and in Hindi, Star is just a percentage point ahead.

That then brings me to the second reason why the IPL seems like a tough bet. The slip in Hindi GECs goes deeper than just sampling changes. As it has grown in size Star has become a large, somewhat bureaucratic company. 'Star values opinion/research but uses so many data points that it slows down decision-making. The team is too huge, sometimes navigating and figuring out who to talk to is challenging. There is too much analysis paralysis. At some point you need to move forward,' says one programme supplier. 'Now they are making stories from the head, not the heart,' says

---

[11] Number of individuals in 000s of a target audience who viewed an 'event', averaged across minutes (from BARC glossary).

another producer who has made shows for Star Plus. 'Research is important but what about instinct or belief. Research said no go to *Saathiya* but it turned out to be a very profitable show. They shelve shows too soon. Somebody's conviction has to drive the show. At Star research doesn't give direction, it makes the decision,' says a former senior manager. 'In any successful show nothing happens for a month. Ratings won't come because characters are not being allowed to be built up,' says one writer. And so on it goes from writers, directors, producers and managers.

It was in anticipation of such a scenario that Shankar had reorganized Star in April 2016 around four business units—entertainment, sports, digital and films—with the help of the Boston Consulting Group. (Shankar has a weakness for blue-chip consulting firms, say colleagues and associates.) 'The reason Star has grown is because we worked well as a close-knit team. Everybody is very capable, all aligned on strategy. For the first five–six years after I took over [in 2007] things were simple. New York set the agenda and the operating targets and I ran the business. We were a large company, but it was mostly about Star Plus and a few other channels, and I was running it totally from the front. And whenever we wanted to do something—sports, regional or Hotstar—we invested in high-quality talent and grew the business. When I joined we had a team of 1100 people. Today, there are 4000 full-timers. And increasingly I feel it is not possible to run with the same approach because of the complexity and size of the business and also because it is not fair to the large number of capable people we have. We need to give space to the entrepreneurial spirit of the organization and ensure that it is not held back by its weight and size,' said Shankar soon after the reorganization was announced.

The idea was the CEO for each of the four businesses would create their own teams and help deepen and widen the pool of talent. 'Also the vision inputs become more diverse. So far the job of thinking has revolved around me and a few others. It will help us take multiple growth initiatives parallelly. We have always taken only one major initiative at a time, sports, regional or Hotstar. Now we don't have the luxury of doing things sequentially,' said Shankar. When there were rumblings of discontent as power structures were realigned, he said: 'We have gone from one CEO to one managing director and four CEOs so there is more space and accountability. A CEO is the owner of the P&L and it is a struggle, people are still coming to terms with it. The whole structure was designed after a fair amount of work and after getting feedback on all the issues involved. Earlier I was on top of all the businesses. But we are growing very fast. For me to keep track of what is happening on say Suvarna or Jalsha [Kannada and Bangla channels] on a daily basis is impossible.'

It is. Which brings us to a question that is best answered in the epilogue: What is Star without Shankar?

Meanwhile, with the entertainment business somewhat challenged and the investment phase ongoing in kabaddi, football and other sports, and in Hotstar, what is Star's flexibility on IPL? The growth in the tournament's TV viewership has slowed down, though online it continues to shoot up. Sony did an average of Rs 1000 crore to Rs 1500 crore ($154 million to $231 million) annually over the ten years that it owned the property. The estimate is that in the first year Star did close to Rs 2000 crore ($307 million). If in five years it manages to reach break-even, it would have achieved a lot.[12] Analysts reckon pay revenues, the one big strength Disney has had in every market it goes to, might be the answer.

Kunal Dasgupta, the former CEO of Sony who made the first audacious bid for an unknown property called the IPL, is sanguine. He reckons, 'Whether the IPL makes money or not doesn't matter because now Disney is in charge. They [Star] wouldn't have spent $2.5 billion unless they knew they would get a $16 billion valuation.'

---

[12] All the dollar–rupee conversions in this paragraph have been done at Rs 65 to a dollar, the rate when Star bid for the IPL in 2017. This is for the sake of consistency in comparison.

The acquisition by Disney

Late in 2017, The Walt Disney Company made a $52.4 billion bid for a bulk of 21st Century Fox's assets. These included its movie studios, television production, regional sports and international businesses, including Star India. Even as Fox accepted and was going through with the first steps, in June 2018 Comcast stepped in. The $94.5 billion Comcast Corporation, the world's second-largest media firm (Alphabet, Google's owner, is the first) offered $65 billion, in cash, for the assets. Within a week, Disney announced that it had signed an amended acquisition agreement with 21st Century Fox upping the bid to $71.3 billion. Much of this corporate drama ended with Fox selling to the $60 billion Disney, which was then the higher bidder.

Of all the things Disney has taken on with the Fox acquisition, the one that has the most potential for growth and expansion is Star India. The deal valued Star India at anywhere between $10 billion and $15 billion, says Couto. Rupert Murdoch's Asia dream was finally valued for what it was—an exciting, high-growth market. What Murdoch saw in Star TV in 1993 is what Disney saw in Fox and in Star in 2018—a way to grow in markets outside of the US.

As Star goes through the steps of becoming a Disney operation, what does the future hold?

Epilogue

What will happen to Star without Shankar?

What will happen after Disney starts running Star?

These are questions I asked many of the 100 interviewees for this book.[1] These are questions many of us analysts and observers ask each other. Take the first one.

Shankar himself has always pooh-poohed any rumours of him quitting or getting bored. 'Every day this company brings me a big problem to solve. How do we build a sports business or a digital business? How to push up Star Plus or grow in other languages?' he said soon after Star won the IPL bid in September 2017. That is true. From an estimated Rs 1600 crore ($400 million) in March 2007 to Rs 13,448 crore ($2.06 billion) in March 2018, from a one-channel firm to a fully fledged media company, he has brought vision and scale to the firm and catapulted it to another league. 'Uday's biggest

---

[1] Not all of them feature in the list in this book. Some chose not to be mentioned.

contribution is that he has driven the business to this point. He is a poker player, he bets all his chips.,' laughs Punit Goenka, managing director and CEO, Zee Entertainment Enterprises. He shares a great rapport with Shankar although they are keen rivals.

Speak to programme producers or consultants outside the company, and they will all tell you stories about how 'Uday-centric' Star is. 'The conversation at Star starts with "what Uday wants". He is clear about what he wants, articulates it and cuts through the crap, particularly in content,' quips one programme supplier who dealt with him during his first few years at Star. While he may not directly handle content now, the description holds. Shankar is an imperious man who has, over eleven years of being CEO, been proved right again and again. This then presents its own problems.

'In Star there is the diwan-e-khaas [hall of private audience] for confidantes and the diwan-e-aam [hall of common audience] for people who are expendable commodities,' says one senior manager who quit. Jacob, Gupta and a handful of people form the diwan-e-khaas. Like many strong personalities, Shankar respects 'people who stand up to him', says one former manager. There were at least half a dozen anecdotes from interviewees on how he actually listened to those who stood up for what they believed in. So success has changed him, but there is still the journalist who enjoys both questioning and being questioned.

Shankar's personality and working style will come under a magnifying glass afresh. By the time you read this, Star will be a Disney firm. That has several ramifications.

Fox is an extremely entrepreneurial, cowboyish company. The Murdochs bet, take risks and don't give a damn what the market thinks. 'Rupert has a lot of charisma, and managers want to go into battle for him,' says Couto. That is not surprising given how far ahead he thinks and how much he backs his people. 'People don't realize what a federal structure we [Fox] work in. If I take a concept to New York it is because I am not sure or because I need money. Working with the Murdochs has spoilt me. The amount of ownership and freedom I have here is tremendous,' Shankar has told me several times. Fox's culture and its fit with Shankar's journalistic bent of mind come from its control by the Murdochs. 'They [Murdochs] leave you alone. James doesn't stop me if he has a different opinion—he puts in his word but says I leave the decision to you,' says Harit Nagpal, CEO and managing director, Tata Sky. Fox has a minority shareholding in the DTH firm.

One reason, as Bruce Churchill says earlier in the chapter 'Star-crossed', is that News Corp is not originally an American company. 'A lot of American companies look at the international markets as a sales opportunity. News Corp started in Australia, then built a successful business in the UK and then went to the US. So we knew we could build an international business by going and building local stuff, we didn't take the Australian papers to the UK. Some of the companies are more guilty of an American approach,' he says. Churchill was with Star in Asia from 1996 to 2004 before moving to DirecTV.

Disney, on the other hand, is a cautious, process-oriented, typically American multinational. 'Disney management is by committees. It slows down the whole thing. They take perfect decisions but perfectly delayed decisions,' says one senior media person. The Walt Disney Company is among the largest media firms in the world at about $60 billion in revenues. That is roughly twice the top line of 21st Century Fox, which does $30.4 billion. In India, though, Star is far bigger—it is about twenty times Disney's size. Disney, which entered India in 1993, around the same time as Star, hasn't done as well. It had one big acquisition, UTV, is a good player in the kids' space and has eight channels and a consumer products business. It shut down its local film studio in 2016. Put Star and Disney together and you get a largely complementary business in India. There is no issue with the strategic fit.

But the cultural differences between the two firms are huge. 'It has one of the most ruthless and brutal management cultures. There will be a huge cultural challenge for News Corp,' says the former CEO of one of the News Corp businesses in India. 'Disney is a very

US-centric company; everything international is about marketing and syndication, it has no creative bones, no risk appetite. If you take that DNA and put it in an entrepreneurial company . . .,' adds another media baron. 'If Disney tries to change the DNA of Star that would be a big mistake,' says Goenka. The other big threat, he reckons, is if the sports bet doesn't pay off.

There is then an interesting bunch of variables coming into play as Star changes hands. There is Shankar's personality, Disney's personality, the Fox DNA and a large number of interesting balls in the air with lots of long-term potential. There is kabaddi, Hotstar, IPL. How would the bets that Shankar made square with Disney's stodgy approach?

Now add one big variable. As I write this in April 2019, Zee is talking to potential buyers to offload 20–25 per cent of the firm. The idea is to get a strategic investor as well as help deleverage some of the holding company Essel's huge debt burden, piled up as a result of Subhash Chandra's ambitious bets on infrastructure. The $94.5 billion Comcast, the world's largest media company, is one of the potential suitors. Whoever buys it, by the end of 2019 Zee's management and part of its ownership too will change. The two largest players in the Rs 1,67,400 crore ($23.9 billion) Indian media and entertainment business won't be who they were at the beginning of 2019.

What could this mean? More consolidation, for one. There could soon be some jostling from Sony and Sun as they try to scale up in a hurry. Second, it will mean a greater focus on building online businesses because the competition for Star or Disney or Zee will increasingly be from Google or Netflix or Tencent or Jio. And the profitable TV business will fund it.

Late in 2018, Disney announced that Shankar would be chairman for Star and Disney India and president APAC, direct-to-consumer and international for The Walt Disney Company. That Shankar was chosen to head a team that includes some big talent across China, Australia, Korea and the Middle East is a testament to what he has achieved. The next few steps, however, will be tough especially without the 'double or quits' mentality of the Murdochs backing Shankar and Star India.

Star thrived first under a Chinese owner and then an Australian one. It will be intriguing to watch what it achieves under this very American one.

Appendices

Appendix A

Star India Revenue and Profit Numbers

21st Century Fox

($ million)	FY10	FY11	FY12	FY13	FY14	FY15	FY16	FY17	FY18
Revenue	32,778	24,232	25,051	27,675	31,867	28,987	27,326	28,500	30,400
EBITDA	5728	4820	5757	6261	6715	6722	6597	7428	7286

Star India

	FY10	FY11	FY12	FY13	FY14	FY15	FY16	FY17	FY18
Exchange Rate (INR/$)	65.0	65.0	65.0	65.0	65.0	65.0	65.0	65.0	65.0
in $ million	FY10	FY11	FY12	FY13	FY14	FY15	FY16	FY17	FY18
Revenue									
Subscription	173.2	205.5	258.2	300.0	333.1	400.2	445.8	440.9	600.2
TV Channels	173.2	205.5	258.2	300.0	333.1	399.2	439.1	422.2	559.1
Digital	0.0	0.0	0.0	0.0	0.0	1.0	6.7	18.7	41.1
Adsales	234.9	310.6	393.8	493.7	561.2	670.9	916.4	908.0	1238.6
TV Channels	234.9	310.6	393.8	493.7	561.2	663.8	892.9	873.1	1151.1
Digital	0.0	0.0	0.0	0.0	0.0	7.1	23.5	34.9	87.5
Syndication	30.8	33.8	36.9	42.3	60.9	99.4	110.3	103.9	185.6
Others	15.6	12.0	15.0	30.8	33.4	44.2	38.0	42.5	44.6
Total Revenue	454.4	561.9	703.9	866.8	988.7	1214.7	1510.5	1495.2	2068.9
Total Costs	419.7	505.2	632.6	797.2	969.1	1267.6	1306.1	1265.9	1616.6
EBITDA	34.6	56.7	71.3	69.6	19.6	-52.9	204.4	229.4	452.3

Star India

in INR million	FY10	FY11	FY12	FY13	FY14	FY15	FY16	FY17	FY18
Revenue									
Subscription	11,255.0	13,360.0	16,780.0	19,500.0	21,650.0	26,015.5	28,980.0	28,658.6	39,011.3
TV Channels	11,255.0	13,360.0	16,780.0	19,500.0	21,650.0	25,948.8	28,544.3	27,443.2	36,338.5
Digital					0.0	66.7	435.8	1215.5	2672.8
Ad Sales	15,268.0	20,186.0	25,600.0	32,089.9	36,479.3	43,609.2	59,564.6	59,018.4	80,508.6
TV Channels	15,268.0	20,186.0	25,600.0	32,089.9	36,479.3	43,145.2	58,036.3	56,748.4	74,821.3
Digital					0.0	464.0	1528.3	2270.0	5687.3
Syndication	2000.0	2200.0	2400.0	2750.0	3959.2	6459.2	7167.0	6753.0	12,063.6
Others	1011.0	779.0	973.0	2002.0	2174.2	28742	2472.0	2760.0	2897.5
Total Revenue	29,534.0	36,525.0	45,753.0	56,341.9	64,262.7	78,958.1	98,183.6	97,190.1	1,34,481.0
Total Costs	27,281.8	32,839.0	41,116.0	51,816.9	62,991.8	82,395.5	84,896.0	82,280.9	1,05,079.8
EBITDA	2252.2	3686.0	4637.0	4524.9	1270.9	-3437.4	13,287.5	14,909.2	29,401.3

Source: Media Partners Asia

Note: EBITDA is earnings before interest, depreciation, taxes and amortization; Media Partners Asia uses a constant exchange rate for historical financials that reflect a reasonable average over these years; Star's revenues are for the year ending March.

Appendix B

The Rise and Rise of India's TV Industry

Year	TV Homes	Revenues (Rs crore)		
		Ad	Pay	Total
1992	35	395	101	496
1993	40	496	252	748
1994	46	848	991	1839
1995	52	1345	1800	3145
1996	58	1975	2160	4135
1998	69	3367	3480	6847
2000	73	4439	3960	8399
2001	79	4794	4800	9594
2002	82	4717	4859	9576
2003	85	5094	8820	13,914
2004	100	5802	9900	15,702
2005	108	6746	11,160	17,906
2006	112	6050	13,176	19,226
2007	117	7110	14,400	21,510

Year	TV Homes	Revenues (Rs crore)		
		Ad	Pay	Total
2008	123	8200	16,740	24,940
2009	123	8800	19,980	28,780
2010	134	10,300	22,860	33,160
2011	141	11,600	25,380	32,800
2012	148	12,480	26,640	37,000
2013	161	13,600	28,100	41,700
2014	168	15,500	32,000	47,500
2015	175	18,100	36,100	54,200
2016	183	20,100	38,700	58,800
2017	183	26,700	39,300	66,000
2018	197	30,500	43,500	74,000

Note: The pay revenues from cable in the initial years are impossible to determine since there are no estimates of how many households were connected. From 1992–94 cable revenues are calculated at Rs 70 per connected household per month. From 1995–2002, they are calculated at Rs 100 per home per month and from thereon at Rs 150. From 2011 onwards, since the gap between only DD homes which do not pay anything and cable and satellite and DTH homes is very low, all TV homes are considered pay homes for the sake of calculating subscription revenues. From this year, all the data comes from FICCI-Frames reports released in the respective years.

Sources: Doordarshan annual reports, Ministry of Information and Broadcasting releases, NRS, Satellite and Cable TV Magazine, Lodestar Media (now Lodestar Universal), TAM Media Research, BARC, TRAI, Zenith Optimedia, FICCI-Frames Reports and The Indian Media Business *(New Delhi: Sage, 2013).*

Data compiled and analysed by Vanita Kohli-Khandekar. This data may be reproduced only with due credit to either The Indian Media Business *or Vanita Kohli-Khandekar.*

Appendix C

India's Top Media Companies

Company/Group	Revenues (Rs crore, FY2018)
Zee Group	13,825
Star	13,448
Times Group*	10,000
Tata Sky	5720
Sony	6500
Network 18	5027
Bharti Airtel (Digital TV)	3757
Sun Network	3105
HT Media	2592
PVR Cinemas	2365

* Estimated

Source: Annual Reports and Company Estimates

Research Resources and Bibliography

1. 21st Century Fox website, annual reports, corporate presentations and conference transcripts.
2. Amit Agarwal, 'Subhash Chandra Makes Television History', *India Today*, 15 August 1994.
3. Amit Agarwal, 'Star TV Targets India with New Programmes and Channels', *India Today*, 30 June 1994.
4. Anupama Chandra and Amit Agarwal, 'Star TV Faces Flak over Provocative Remarks on Nikki Tonight Talk Show', *India Today*, 31 May 1995.
5. BARC website and data, 2015 onwards.
6. Broadband Asia archives, 2000.
7. *Businessworld* archives, 2000–07, courtesy of Anurag Batra, owner of *BW: Businessworld*.
8. *Business Standard* archives, 2009–18.
9. C.A. Mason, 'A Case Study of Rupert Murdoch: Paradigm or Maverick?', September 1992, a master's thesis submitted to Loughborough University Institutional Respository.

10. Cable and Satellite Asia archives, 1993–2000.
11. EY and KPMG's reports for FICCI-Frames.
12. Faheem Ruhani, 'What Led Aamir Khan to Do a Show like *Satyamev Jayate*', *India Today*, 28 August 2014.
13. https://www.asiasat.com/news/blog/blog-title-2.
14. Jason Nisse and Teresa, 'When the Stardust Finally Settled: Rupert Murdoch's Coup in Snatching Hong Kong's Satellite TV Station', *Independent*, 1 August 1993.
15. Jemima Hunt, 'How a Bombay Mix Put the Heat on MTV', *Independent*, 1 October 1996.
16. Jonathan Karp, 'News Corp to Sell Its Stakes in Indian TV to Zee Telefilms', *Wall Street Journal*, 27 September 1999.
17. Kathryn Harris, 'Is Murdoch's Empire Living on Borrowed Time?', *Los Angeles Times*, 18 October 1992.
18. Linda Keslar, 'News Corp PPV venture in the works', *Variety*, 8 October 1992.
19. Louis Kraar, 'A Billionaire's Global Strategy', *Fortune*, 13 July 1992.
20. Luisa Tam, 'News Buys Star TV', *South China Morning Post*, 27 July 1993.
21. Media Partners Asia data and archives, 2001–18.
22. Rajiv Desai, *Indian Business Culture* (Woburn, MA: Butterworth-Heinemann, 1999).
23. 'Rathikant Basu: Utterly Unusual', Shailaja Chandra's Blog, 8 November 2013, over2shailaja.wordpress.com.
24. Ravi Tej Sharma, 'Corporate Bigwigs Like Anand Mahindra, Piyush Pandey and Rajiv Luthra Join Hands to Launch Pro Kabaddi League', *ET Bureau*, 15 March 2014.
25. Reserve Bank of India archives for the rate of the dollar versus the rupee.
26. Richard Covington, 'Music Channels Enlist Big Allies', *New York Times*, 9 June 1995.
27. Ronnie Screwvala, *Dream with Your Eyes Open* (New Delhi: Rupa, 2015).
28. Sean Kennedy, 'Mogul Takes All of Star', *South China Morning Post*, 19 July 1995.
29. Sky Global prospectus.
30. Sky Group website.

31. Subhash Chandra with Pranjal Sharma, *The Z Factor: My Journey As the Wrong Man at the Right Time* (Noida: HarperCollins, 2016).

32. TAM Media Research data, 2000–15.

33. Telecom Regulatory Authority of India research papers, consultation papers and guidelines.

34. *The Hindu*, Star Applies Afresh for Uplinking', 23 September 2003.

35. *The Hindu BusinessLine*, 'Star to Dilute Equity in UTV; Hooks Strategic Ties', 18 March 2000.

36. *The Hindu BusinessLine*, 'DTH, Private FM . . . I&B Ministry Goes Full Throttle on Reforms', 28 December 2000.

37. 'The Dhoni Effect', EY report, March 2008.

38. Tim McGirk, 'Gandhi Gaffe Dims Murdoch's Star', *Independent*, 6 July 1995.

39. Transcript: Goldman Sachs, Communacopia Conference with Joseph P. Nallen, senior EVP and CFO 21CF, 13 September 2018.

40. Vanita Kohli-Khandekar, *The Indian Media Business* (New Delhi: Sage, 2013).

41. *Variety*, 'The Star TV Fleet', 3 April 1995.

42. Zee Entertainment Enterprises Limited's legal department.

Interviews

A huge thank you to all the people who shared their experiences, thoughts and insights on Star or the Indian market with me. Many of these people spoke to me over two sittings. I may not have quoted everyone, but every interview was invaluable.

Ajay Patadia

Ajay Vidyasagar

Ajit Thakur

Anand Mahindra

Ashok Venkatramani

Bimla Bhalla

Bruce Churchill

Charu Sharma

Danish Khan

David Haslingden

Deepak Jacob

Dilshad Master-Kumar

Donald Atyeo

Ed Sharples

Ekta Kapoor

Farokh Balsara

Gary Davey

Gaurav Gandhi

Harit Nagpal

Indira Mansingh

Iqbal Malhotra

Jagdish Kumar

Janine Stein

John O'Loan

Jules Fuller

Kaushal Dalal

Kunal Dasgupta

Mandar Thakur

Meenakshi Menon

Megha Tata

Monika Shergill

Myleeta Aga

Nachiket Pantvaidya

Nitin Kukreja

Nitin Vaidya

Pankaj Raj

Paritosh Joshi

Partho Dasgupta

Prannoy Roy

Punit Goenka

R.C. Venkateish

Raghav Bahl

Raian Karanjawala

Raj Nayak

Rajan Shahi

Rajeev Chandrashekar

Rajesh Kamat

Rajesh Shah

Rakesh Sharma

Rathikant Basu

Ravish Kumar

Richard Dovey

Ronnie Screwvala

Roshan Abbas

Sameer Nair

Satyajit Bhatkal

Shashanka Ghosh

Siddhartha Ray

Siddhartha Basu

Sonali Thakker

Srini Sreeramaneni

Subhash Chandra

Sumantro Dutta

Sumeet Mittal

Sunaman Sood

Sunil Doshi

Sunil Lulla

Sunil Taldar

Sunita Rajan

Tarun Katial

Team Patna Pirates

Todd Miller

Tony D'Silva

Uday Shankar

Vikram Kaushik

Vikram Mehra

Vikram Sakhuja

Vivek Bahl

Vivek Couto

Yash Khanna

Zama Habib